TORPEDOES AWAY!

D0765020

TORPEDOES AWAY!

OUR SUBMARINE NAVY IN THE PACIFIC

MAXWELL HAWKINS

Combat Books
2020

Torpedoes Away! Our Submarine Navy in the Pacific by Maxwell Hawkins.

Published 2020 by Combat Books.

This book or any portion thereof may not be reproduced or used in any manner whatsoever without the express written permission of the publisher except for the use of brief quotations in a book review or scholarly journal.

All rights reserved.

First printing, 2020.

ISBN: 9798608216176.

1 - War

LATE IN NOVEMBER 1941, a tall, well-built lieutenant commander moved along a dock at Pearl Harbor in the direction of the Flag Office of Rear Admiral Thomas Withers, Commander of Submarines, Pacific Fleet. His officer's cap rested at a suitable seagoing angle over his sandy hair—hair that was thinning slightly on top and touched with gray at the temples. He walked with a barely perceptible rolling gait, bent forward a little at the waist; the indelible mark of a man to whom a tilting deck is level and only the land unsteady.

At the Flag Office, he was greeted by Captain C. W. Styer, Chief of Staff to Admiral Withers, who handed him his orders. Then Captain Styer delivered verbally a message from the Admiral.

"Admiral Withers was sorry he couldn't be here when you called," the Chief of Staff said, "but he was detained elsewhere. He wanted me to impress on you, however, that in his opinion we will be at war before you return from this patrol."

With this unequivocal warning in mind, the sandy-haired officer retraced his steps from the Flag Office to the ship he commanded—more than three hundred feet of deadly modern submarine. Lines were cast off, and shortly one of our newer and larger submarines, the *USS Trout*, was slipping through the channel toward the entrance of Pearl Harbor. Once outside, she headed west. Her nose dipped into the long Pacific swells; rising and falling with it on either side were twin rows of huge torpedoes, several of them destined for Japanese hulls.

The captain of the *Trout* was Lieutenant Commander Frank W. Fenno. In the months ahead, his ship was to write some of the most amazing pages in the history of submarine warfare.

The submarine *Trout* was at sea dumping garbage. This would appear to be menial work for an undersea fighting craft that cost around six million dollars, but it was an accommodation to the inhabitants of Midway Islands. In no way was the big gray submarine compromising her dignity or slipping into the category of a garbage scow.

Midway was only a group of empty atolls in the Pacific Ocean until Pan American Airways picked the spot in 1935 for a principal clipper way station and fueling depot on its transpacific air route. From this, Midway developed into an important outpost of our national defense; how important was brought home to the American people on June 4, 1942, when the pride and might of Japan's navy was sent reeling back toward Tokyo in the battle to which Midway gave its name. In the opinion of some authorities, this battle marked the turning point of the war and saved Hawaii, and possibly our West Coast, from a Japanese invasion attempt.

By December 1941, Midway was bustling with activity; Marines, Army and Navy personnel, and construction workers swarmed over the limited area.

Sanitation was one of the problems, and to keep the beaches clean, refuse was hauled well out to sea and dumped where the currents wouldn't sweep it back in. Some of the ships that put in there customarily performed this chore. On this occasion Fenno's immaculate submarine, built to scourge her foes, had volunteered to scavenge for her friends. She pulled out of Midway on December 6, over a calm sea and beneath a peaceful sky, and cruised to a point some twenty miles southwest on her garbage mission. Having dumped the Midway refuse overboard, she continued about her principal business, which was a routine patrol.

That night, the American submarine cruised on the surface, charging her "can," as submariners call the huge storage batteries which supply electric power to operate an undersea craft when it is submerged. Her can fully charged, Fenno's submarine dove at dawn, in accordance with wartime procedure, even though we were not yet at war. In the control room below the conning tower, Lieutenant Albert Clark was in charge of the diving. The control room is the mechanical brain of the submarine, the place from which all its maneuvers are directed. From this central location the communication system reaches out to all parts of the ship; the maze of glistening levers, buttons, valves and other gadgets controls the progress of a submarine in its three-dimensional element.

In a surface ship, the matter of trim is a minor source of concern. Operating in a flat two-dimensional range, the surface vessel offers only the problems of fore and aft and lateral trim, factors which are provided for in construction and loading. Once fixed, only under unusual circumstances are they disturbed. A submarine, however, not only must be trimmed fore and aft and laterally, but also vertically— her depth controlled—and all these factors are inseparably bound together. The depth control of a submarine depends on her various water ballast tanks and valves, and it is maintained by flooding or blowing out these tanks as conditions demand. Trim is of supreme importance in a submarine's operations once she has slipped beneath the surface of the sea. Loss of trim is likely to cause loss of depth control; loss of depth control is likely to result in the craft broaching, breaking through the surface. Consequences of this may be merely embarrassing to the diving officer, or they may be fatal to both submarine and crew if the enemy happens to be attacking at the time.

The officer in charge of the diving is performing just about the most important job in a submarine. With Lieutenant Clark that Sunday morning was the *Trout*'s captain, Lieutenant Commander Fenno, known as Mike throughout the Submarine Service. The enlisted men on watch were standing at their stations with the quiet alertness that submarine duty demands. Farther aft in his cubbyhole adjacent to the control room, the radioman, headphones clamped to his ears, was taking down a message coming over the airwaves.

There was nothing unusual about that scene down under the waters of the Pacific. It had been like that hundreds of times before.

Nothing indicated that this Sunday morning would be any different from the many others spent diving the big American submarine.

Suddenly the radioman slipped the headphones off, eased out of his seat and emerged from his nest of dials and tubes. He came directly to Fenno, as if he were making a routine report.

"A message just came for you, Cap'n," the radioman said.

Fenno broke off his conversation with Clark and walked aft to the radio room with Sparks. Nobody paid much attention to them since there was nothing out of the ordinary in their actions. But in the radio room, Sparks handed the submarine's skipper the most important message ever flashed to American warships. It was Admiral Kimmel's war dispatch to the Pacific Fleet.

THE JAPANESE HAVE RAIDED PEARL HARBOR...

Fenno studied the message. Finally, he glanced at the radioman and said, "Looks like the real thing."

"Yes, Cap'n, it does," Sparks replied.

Still pondering over the dispatch, Mike Fenno returned to the control room. He moved to Clark's side. "Well, Al," he said, "we're at war with Japan! The Japs have just raided Pearl Harbor!"

Clark was from Saco, Maine, and had more than a touch of Yankee skepticism in his makeup. He took his gaze from the depth gauges and gave Fenno a faint grin.

"They have one of those raid tests there every Sunday morning," he said dryly.

Mike Fenno shook his head. The warning he had received at the Flag Office of Admiral Withers only a couple of weeks before never had been far from his thoughts. Besides, the dispatch in his hand permitted no misinterpretation. He held it out so Clark could look at it. "See for yourself," he said. "It's plain enough in this message. As far as I'm concerned, we're at war!"

The American submarine had been on a war footing for months. She was ready for it. There was little to do beyond informing the crew of what had happened. Let them know that the practice days were over. The marbles game was for keeps. No more water-filled exercise heads on their torpedoes. It was warheads, crammed with high explosives, from then on.

Fenno walked aft to the galley, between the control room and the crew's quarters. The cook was busy getting breakfast in his kitchenette.

"As the crew come in for breakfast," the submarine's skipper said easily, "tell 'em we're at war with Japan."

The cook's jaw fell open. For a moment no sound came forth, but then he found his voice.

"Yes, sir," he gulped.

For the next half hour, Fenno and Clark, in the mechanical labyrinth of the control room, discussed Admiral Kimmel's message, speculating on what had happened at Pearl Harbor. Finally, Mike Fenno went aft and looked into the messroom. Some of the boys, their breakfast out of the way, were sitting at the mess table playing cards.

The submarine's captain gave the cardplayers a good looking over. Then he took a deep breath. "We go to war—and you birds play cards!" he exclaimed.

With that, the skipper withdrew. But in telling about the incident, he said that after he had left he began to think it over and saw it from a different angle.

"Well, why not?" he asked himself. "It's a good way to relax. And it's a good sign; shows how cool they are."

Although the crew may have been hiding their excitement, nevertheless the first-day jitters were stalking the deck and almost cost the submarine her captain. The ship was running on the surface. On the bridge, besides the several enlisted men on watch, were Fenno and Lieutenant Fritz Harlfinger. It occurred to the captain that it might be a good time to have a practice drill, so he decided to have the alarm for "battle stations" sounded. The signal for this is a loud gong which rings twelve times. It's carried to every corner of the ship over the loudspeaker system.

With the first stroke, all hands leap to their combat posts. Everybody from the messboy up has one. The diving alarm on a submarine is another ear-shattering signal, consisting of two raucous blasts on a klaxon-like device. Nobody can miss it. And nobody topside wastes a second getting down the hatch into the conning tower, because at the first vibration of the diving alarm, the submarine starts to dive.

In a quick dive—what those outside the Submarine Service call a "crash" dive—it takes from twenty to thirty seconds to submerge. And virtually every dive is a quick dive in war. So there isn't much time for a half dozen men to get through a single twenty-three-inch hatch, and either you get below—or you're "left in the pool." They don't wait and they don't go back in a submarine. Both battle-station and diving alarms are sounded from the bridge by large push buttons, which are fairly close together.

"I passed the word to sound the alarm for battle stations," Fenno said. "But someone was jittery. Instead, the diving alarm was sounded. Before we knew it, we were starting to submerge. There was a wild scramble to clear the deck—get down the hatch.

"I was last. Fritz Harlfinger was ahead of me by a split second. He's small and wiry. Weighs about one-fifty. But as we went down the ladder, I was riding his shoulders all the way, like the Little Old Man of the Sea. And I had the sea right with me! We managed to close the hatch before more than a little of it spilled in, but even that water was too close for comfort."

When the Japanese task force swept in to shell Midway, the *Trout* was too far away to get at it, and the islands themselves lay between. Helplessly those aboard the submarine listened to the distant boom of guns, saw the lashes against the sky, which some of the crew mistook for lightning. Although they promptly maneuvered to be in a position to intercept a second attack, it failed to occur.

January found the American submarine back in Pearl Harbor. So far, she had sunk no enemy ships. The area of her patrol had been poor hunting grounds; she hadn't flushed any Nipponese game. But Fenno's fortunes were soon to change.

The *Trout*'s captain was summoned to the Flag Office, and this time Admiral Withers was there. He gave orders for a pressing and dangerous mission, a mission which at that time was unusual for a submarine. Fenno's undersea warship was to deliver sixty tons of sorely needed shells to the island fortress of Corregidor at the entrance to Manila Bay, in the Philippines.

"Get out there just as fast as you can," Admiral Withers said. "But on your way back, if you want to, it'll be all right to do a little hunting."

A destroyed Vindicator at Ewa field

2 – From Garbage to Glory

LIEUTENANT COMMANDER FENNO'S MISSION to Corregidor was a call for speed and more speed. The shells, taking the place of ballast normally carried by the submarine, were rushed aboard, and supplies, too, were hurried in. The wives of the Submarine Service cast about for something they could do for the valiant men in the Philippines. They had a small fund which was used to buy little luxuries for, or otherwise, help, the enlisted personnel, and they drew on this to purchase eight hundred dollars' worth of cigarettes. These, too, were stowed aboard.

With her contrasting cargo of bad news for the Japanese and good cheer for the men fighting them, the submarine *Trout* slipped out of Pearl Harbor.

"My one worry," said Fenno, "was what to substitute for ballast after I'd dropped those sixty tons of shells at Corregidor. Of course, I figured they'd probably have plenty of sandbags there, and in a pinch I could use them. But you don't like to do that. They get your ship all dirty."

Mike Fenno's comment on getting sand in his submarine typifies the attitude of the present-day submarine captain—or enlisted man, for that matter—toward the state of cleanliness of his ship. To call a modern submarine a pig-boat is an anachronism. It's like calling a Superfortress an egg crate. And don't refer to a submarine as a "sewer pipe" because of the faint aroma of diesel oil that sometimes clings to the clothing of the crew after they've been submerged a long time. No longer does either of these ancient slurs have any foundation of fact. In general, submarines today, throughout their gleaming jungle of machinery and instruments, are kept spotless.

This particular submarine, her captain pondering over the matter of ballast, pushed ever westward toward the beleaguered Philippines. Not since Dr. Rudolf Diesel of Munich invented the oil engine named for him and one of them first was installed in a submarine around 1912, had diesels been called on to propel a ship on a stranger voyage than the one that lay ahead.

The officers represented a good cross-section of the United States. Fenno was from Westminster, Massachusetts; Clark from Saco, Maine; Harlfinger from Albany, New York. The submarine's diving officer was Lieutenant F. A. ("Pop") Gunn, from Kansas City, Missouri, and her communications officer was Ensign Harry E. Woodward, from the state of Washington. The commissary officer was Ensign Ray Pitts, USNR.

The seventh officer was Lieutenant (j.g.) George Schottler, USNR, from Baltimore, an ROTC graduate of Georgia Tech.

Fenno's submarine drove into the Pacific waters at its best speed, which it could attain above, and not under, the ocean. The *Trout* was traversing waters controlled to a large extent by the enemy, but her luck was good and for a considerable part of her journey the sea was her exclusive property.

"Then one night," Fenno said, "we picked up a steady light ahead." He smiled faintly. "I knew the crew wouldn't like it if I passed up a chance to sink a Jap ship. So I decided to investigate."

It was a dark night, with low-hanging clouds, ideal for a surface attack. The American submarine moved cautiously forward. On the bridge, all eyes were straining to penetrate the darkness. Closer and closer they slipped through the gentle Pacific swells. At last they were within range. One torpedo leaped from the submarine's bow. There was a long, tense wait. But nothing happened.

The submarine continued to press ahead until she was scarcely five hundred yards away from the mysterious light. At that point, those topside discovered it came from a Japanese patrol boat; and at the same time, the enemy discovered the submarine.

"We'd stuck our neck out," Fenno related ruefully. "That Jap started right after us. We made a quick dive. After about an hour, I decided to come up for a look around. This time there were a lot of lights ahead. The Jap patrol boats were signaling to each other."

The *Trout* had met the enemy, but she couldn't afford to stick around for a decision fight. There was an important date to be kept out there in the Philippines, where the Americans and Filipinos were beginning to battle with their backs to the wall. So Mike Fenno maneuvered his ship around the nest of enemy patrol boats and proceeded on his course.

Later, in the South China Sea, Fenno had occasion to remember that unblinking light he encountered on his way to Corregidor—and then he had time to do something about it. The shell-laden submarine reached her rendezvous on time, was led through the minefields and soon was unloading her deadly cargo at Corregidor even faster than she had put it aboard at Pearl Harbor. Added incentive was dropping from the skies out there in the far Pacific—Japanese bombs, and lots of them!

The Japanese by this time had complete mastery of the air and were raiding steadily. The submarine had to lie on the bottom of the harbor during the day for protection; only at night could unloading operations be carried out.

"I was still wondering what to do about ballast," Fenno said, "and began to make a few inquiries about getting some sandbags. It looked as if that was all I could get. But finally they told me that if ballast was what I was looking for, they'd give me something a lot better than sand." He laughed.

"The first thing we knew, a flock of trucks began to arrive. We could hardly believe our eyes when we saw that they were loaded with gold! And silver!"

With feverish speed, the crew of the *Trout* and the soldiers of Corregidor unloaded the treasure from the trucks. The gold was in heavy, gleaming bars; the silver was in coins, packed in canvas bags. Panting and sweating, the men lugged the precious metal into the submarine and stowed it in the space that had been occupied by the brass and steel shells. Beneath a waning Manila moon, they tugged and heaved. Standard bars of gold and bags of silver coins are heavy.

"We worked like mad to get that stuff aboard so we could shove off before it got light," Fenno said. "It was a hot spot for a submarine.

"The bags the silver was in must have been lying in vaults a long time because some of them had rotted. They broke while we were carrying them. Money was rolling all over the pier, dropping through cracks and splashing into the water.

"One of the crew said he'd never in his life expected to let so much money slip through his fingers. They were all laughing and making cracks about our 'ballast,' but working like the dickens to get it loaded."

Before dawn they won their race against time and the Japanese bombers. The *Trout* cast off her lines and headed toward the minefields guarding the harbor entrance. Enough lights were turned on to enable the guide boat to get her bearings and lead the gold-filled submarine safely through. Probably not since the days of the Spanish treasure fleets has a ship put to sea with such bizarre and valuable ballast. In addition to the many bags of silver, there were twenty-five tons of gold bars. All told, the metal in the hold of Mike Fenno's submarine represented about twenty-five million dollars!

"Before we got through," Fenno said, "I would have swapped it all for a few more torpedoes." And he meant it. Admiral Withers' permission to Fenno to do a little enemy-hunting after delivering the shells offered an opportunity no submarine skipper could turn down, gold or no gold. So after he left Corregidor, Fenno headed up toward Formosa, or Taiwan, as the Japanese called it.

The *Trout* poked her nose northward through the waters of the South China Sea. But not until several days out did she encounter anything, and then it was a typhoon; one of the worst storms Fenno had ever experienced. The submarine fought mountainous waves and terrific winds.

It was impossible even to get a bearing. For four days, the captain admitted, they weren't sure where they were. The only certain thing was that they were still afloat and thankful for it.

Eventually the storm passed, and the doughty American submarine, shaken but intact, arrived in the vicinity of Formosa.

The *Trout* had begun by pinch-hitting for a garbage scow. Then she had been cast in the dual role of munitions transport and bearer of gifts. Her next assignment made her a treasure ship, by accident. But now she was to come into her own, to fulfill the destiny for which she had been built.

It was a bright moonlight night. The sea was rocky from the storm, the kind of water that operates to the advantage of a submarine, because it makes periscopes hard to spot.

The *Trout* was cruising on the surface, everybody topside peering across the tumbling, moonlit waves in the hope of catching the faint smudge of an approaching ship.

They knew they were in an area where enemy shipping could be expected over the horizon at any moment. But it was from below decks that the quarry was detected. The man on watch at the listening gear picked up the sound of a ship's screw. The moon was too bright for a surface attack, so the submarine dove and waited. It wasn't long before Fenno at the periscope saw the enemy vessel, a freighter, coming right across the *Trout's* course.

The air within the round, gray hull of the submarine was charged with suppressed excitement. At their battle stations, the crew were tense and quiet. His blue eyes fixed on the image of the approaching ship in the periscope, Fenno passed the order to make ready two of the bow torpedo tubes. In the forward room the torpedomen moved quickly and expertly, and in a moment the word came back to the control room that two "tin fish" were ready for launching, except for opening the outer doors of the tubes. At the firing circuits, the chief of the boat, the top-ranking enlisted man in a submarine, spoke to the captain.

"Tubes ready, sir."

There was a brief pause as Fenno lined up the unsuspecting Nipponese freighter. Then his crisp voice broke the silence.

"Stand by one!"

At the fire control panel, the chief of the boat turned a key that connected the firing circuit with tube No. 1 and cut out the others. Fenno's command had gone to all parts of the ship over the battle phone system. In the forward torpedo room the torpedo gang were poised to fire the tube by hand should anything go wrong with the electric firing circuit.

"One's ready!" the chief announced.

The *Trout's* captain took a final calculating look at the oncoming target.

"Fire one!" he ordered.

The chief's right hand moved a few inches, pushed the button of the firing circuit. There was a faint thud, a gentle quiver that ran the length of the craft, as the torpedo sped from its tube through the waters of the South China Sea.

The bow planesman had already set the planes to "hard dive," in order to compensate for the weight of the fired torpedo and keep the submarine's bow from being forced upward. In the torpedo room a torpedoman had jerked up the vent that flooded the empty tube with sea water to maintain the ship's trim.

"One's gone!" the chief exclaimed. At the same time, his left hand manipulated the keys that cut out tube No. 1 and cut in tube No. 2. "Two's ready!"

As the first torpedo with its explosive-laden warhead churned toward the enemy, the sixty-odd men in the submarine waited with tightened throats. The seconds ticked by slowly, and they thought of that time on the way to Corregidor, when nothing had happened. But at last there came a dull, muffled boom. Instantly the tension snapped.

It was a hit! First blood for the *Trout*. Some of the men cheered and some pounded each other on the back. "The freighter was making about ten knots," Fenno said. "She was such a pushover, I almost felt sorry for her. That first fish slowed her down to about three knots. I decided to poke her with another." He gave the order:

"Fire two!"

Again the chief's hand pressed the firing circuit.

"Two's gone!" he announced. "Torpedoes away, sir!" Fenno nodded slightly. "Secure the tubes!" Once more the crew waited in grim expectancy and hope as the second big torpedo leaped from the *Trout*'s bow. A second muffled explosion told them they had scored twice. Mike Fenno's description of the result was a combination of modesty and satisfaction. His feelings were plain, but all he said was: "Down she went!" The *Trout* under Fenno had bagged the first of a long string of Japanese ships that she eventually sent to the bottom. After that she continued to patrol the area without success for some time. Then, one night, dead ahead, appeared the fixed light of a patrol boat. The captain's thoughts immediately swung back to his experience with that other light on the way out to Corregidor, but he kept his submarine pushing steadily forward.

"I was expecting them to start shooting any minute," he said. "But they didn't. We dove and picked up the light through the periscope."

Slowly and cautiously, the *Trout* eased in. Finally the order came to fire one torpedo. At their battle stations the crew held their breath, waiting for the dull explosion that would tell them they had hit the target. The blast of a torpedo when heard aboard a submarine is sometimes described as like the distant sound of a boiler blowing up.

No such heartening noise came to the straining ears of the crew. On the contrary, the sound man caught something that was definitely disconcerting—the whir of a torpedo, not their own, boiling past them.

Instantly the American ship went down deeper. Again the listening gear picked up the harrowing sound of an enemy torpedo—and it passed right at the spot where the submarine had been a moment before. The *Trout* struck back with another torpedo herself. But fired under such difficult conditions, it also missed. For a long time the men listened trying to get on a steady bearing. When Fenno decided they had what they wanted, they took a third shot at the Japanese ship.

"That time," he said with great relish, "we made aviators out of those Japs on the patrol boat. Blew it all to splinters!"

The *Trout* had done more than sink another Nipponese craft. She had destroyed the bait of an enemy trap. The trick was—and the submariners knew it well—to have one patrol boat shine a fixed light, an easy target for a submarine, while a second patrol boat lay in wait at one side for any unwary attacker. This was one time the trick didn't work; Mike Fenno's ship, with its millions of dollars' worth of gold and silver, pulled clear of immediate danger and continued her hunt for more Japanese.

Not long after this the Americans had to return to their home waters. They were due back in Pearl Harbor on a certain date, so they headed eastward.

"On the way," Fenno said, "I figured out a good joke. When we pulled into Pearl Harbor, I was going to put a group of the boys around the mess table and have them playing poker. They would use stacks of silver coins and gold bars from our ballast as chips. Then I was going to call in some of my friends and show them how much money we had made in the Pacific ..."

He shook his head sadly. "It didn't work out. We had to get that gold on its way to the mainland as fast as we could, and there was no time for kidding." The *Trout* kept a secret rendezvous with a cruiser and transferred her gold and silver to the larger ship, which brought it to the United States.

The courageous voyage of the *Trout* to Corregidor with sixty tons of shells, and her almost fantastic trip home with a ballast of bullion and a couple of sinkings on the way, received official recognition. Admiral Withers gave letters of commendation to all the officers and enlisted men. The Army awarded the Distinguished Service Cross to Fenno and the Silver Star to all the other officers and all the members of the crew. Captain Fenno also received the Navy Cross, which is the highest fleet decoration, outranked only by the Congressional Medal of Honor. And this was only the beginning of his career in the war; later exploits won him still further decorations.

For the *Trout*, too, the patrol to Corregidor was only the beginning. She was still to sink many Japanese ships; to pick half-drowned Japanese prisoners from the sea; to tote torpedoes right into Japan's front yard and plant them in enemy ships under the noses of the Japanese on shore.

USS Trout (SS-202)

3 – Hard Like Duty

EVEN UNDER THE MOST FAVORABLE CIRCUMSTANCES, life in a submarine is not easy. Aside from the hazards of navigating beneath the surface of the sea, either in peace or in war, submarine duty imposes an abnormal strain on the nervous system. It involves great physical hardship and an environment which prevents proper exercise. Neither of these conditions contributes to good health.

The Navy long has recognized this. For years, service in the submarines has been designated as "hard-line duty" for which additional pay is given. At the present time the men in our submarines, both officers and enlisted personnel, receive an extra fifty percent added to their base pay. Because of this and the fact that almost every enlisted man in a submarine has a petty officer rating of some kind, submarine crews are probably the most prosperous of our sea fighters. They deserve all they get.

A civilian, in order to obtain a real idea of the cramped conditions under which our submariners eat and sleep, work and play, must first understand what their ships are. One of our modern submarines cruising on the surface presents a slim and racy appearance. The topside is only about fifteen feet wide where the conning tower rises. It tapers forward to the bow, and it also tapers to a point at the stern. But its appearance is deceptive, as far as the like. actual structure of the craft is concerned. There's much more to a submarine than meets the eye. Beneath this slim deck with the contours of a racing shell, the submarine swells out into a round fat hull, or, more exactly, two hulls. In a way, it is a ship within a ship. It has an outer hull and an inner, or pressure, hull; between them are the ballast tanks which regulate the craft's buoyancy by inducting or expelling sea water. It is by means of adding or subtracting the weight of this water that the submarine is able to dive and surface, although large planes at the bow and stern, somewhat like a fish's fins, help to control this operation and make it less difficult.

The highest point on a modern submarine, aside from the periscope, is a lookout platform which is above and a little aft of the bridge. Below the bridge is the conning tower, and when you crawl through its twenty-three-inch hatchway and down the ladder you arrive amidships in the belly of the submarine, in its most important compartment, the control room.

While different classes of submarines vary in their layout, and even submarines in the same class are subject to minor changes while building, this is the general plan of the new ships that tore Japan's navy and merchant fleet to pieces.

There are eight compartments below decks divided from each other by steel partitions, or bulkheads, each pierced by a single oval doorway. When you pass through these doorways, you step high and bend low, because they are barely large enough for an ordinary-sized man to go through.

They are airtight and when necessary they can be closed and any one compartment sealed up. Nearest the bow inside a submarine is the bulkhead containing the breech doors of the bow torpedo tubes.

Extending aft is the forward torpedo room, in which are carried extra torpedoes. Part of the crew also sleep here in ingeniously designed rollaway metal-pipe berths. The fact that some of them fit snugly over gleaming torpedoes containing hundreds of pounds of TNT doesn't worry real submarine men. Also in the forward torpedo room is the delicate and secret listening device, or sound gear, as it is generally called. By means of this complicated supersonic instrument, the submarine is able to pick up underwater noises ranging from the crunching of fish jaws to the throbbing roar of a battleship's propellers. The man at the sound gear—the soundman—not only can distinguish the type of ship he hears by differences in the vibrations of various propellers, but also can estimate the speed at which the vessel is moving by counting the revolutions per minute.

The usefulness of this listening apparatus in successful submarine operation cannot be overemphasized. Squeezing through the oval bulkhead door, you enter the forward battery room. There are no batteries in it. It receives its name from the fact that some of the huge storage batteries that drive the ship when it is underwater are placed directly below its deck. The forward battery room is crossed by a narrow passageway off which are a number of small rooms. These include the cabins in which the officers sleep, the wardroom, and some undersized telephone booths which the petty officer staff uses as offices.

The wardroom is the largest of these compartments; but there is just enough room around its dining table for eight men to be seated, three on a side and one at each end. Nevertheless, the wardroom contains cleverly designed cupboards for linen and silver, a shelf holding the submarine's library, a record player, a telephone at the captain's place, and other compactly arranged comforts and necessities. At the forward side is a waist-high partition separating it from a pantry, which has a small electric stove and refrigerator and enough room for a mess attendant to turn around.

The officers' sleeping quarters contain upper and lower bunks, steel washbowls, racks for clothing, and a couple of lockers for personal possessions. When the bunks are occupied, the cabins are just about filled up. The captain, as befits his rank, is housed a little better, although he frequently shares his luxury with another officer, who gets the upper bunk. The captain's cabin is all of six feet square. In addition to the conveniences of the other cabins, it also has a nice assortment of instruments illuminated by indirect lighting. Among them are a depth gauge, a gyrocompass dial, and a brace of telephones. The weary submarine captain can open one eye and tell at a glance what his ship is doing and where it is with reference to the top or the bottom of the ocean.

Cramped and compact though all these quarters are, they are always spotless, gleaming with green paint and stainless-steel trim, which is both practical and decorative. In the wardroom one sits on comfortable cushions of artificial leather. If the general effect is a little reminiscent of some of our modernistic soda fountains, certainly few submarine officers object. It's easy to keep the quarters neat, and that's the way they are kept.

Go through another bulkhead and you're in the control room. This compartment is the general headquarters of the ship, to use an Army term. Directly above the control room in the conning tower, the captain has his post in battle and issues his orders, which are transmitted throughout the submarine by signals, phone, or even word of mouth if necessary.

The most conspicuous thing in the control room is the periscope, which is about in the center of the compartment. It also can be used from the conning tower above. At the periscope the skipper watches what is taking place on the surface of the sea when his ship is submerged, provided it isn't below periscope depth.

The entire control room is filled with apparatus which—as the name indicates—controls the submarine. There are countless gauges, indicators and controls, among them a supersonic fathometer, which is the modern substitute for the lead plummet with which soundings were made in the old days. The fathometer is a device which projects a sound wave and by timing the return of the echo, the depth of water under the ship's keel can be determined. In the maneuvering room farther aft are the engine and electric motor controls. In the conning tower is the panel of electric buttons to fire the torpedoes.

From the control room the diving planes, the compressed-air manifolds, and the pumps are manipulated. On the wall is a large indicator board on which a system of lights shows the position of every vent and valve in the submarine. This board is called the "Christmas tree," since the lights are red and green—the former to indicate open and the latter to indicate shut. Add some electric meters, fuse boards, a gyrocompass, steering apparatus, and a chart table for the navigation officer, and you have a partial picture of the mechanical jungle that makes up a control room.

Aft of the control room is the galley, where the food for both officers and crew is prepared. Adjoining is the messroom, which can accommodate only about half the crew at a time. These spaces sometimes are called the kitchenette and the dinette. The cook sets a first and second table. Beneath the messroom are ice machines and refrigerated storage rooms for meats, frozen foods and vegetables, as well as storerooms for other foods and the ammunition magazine.

Beyond the messroom is a section known as the crew space. About half the enlisted men sleep here, on bunks with metal springs. Each man also has a small locker.

They do not have much personal room, because there isn't much to be had. Adjoining the crew space are a washroom and several shower baths. You have to make up your mind which way to stand before you go into the showers because of their small size. If you walk in face first, you may have to back out; but if you back in, you're pointed in the right direction for a quick exit.

On some of the boats, flushing the toilet when a submarine is beneath the surface is one of the most complicated operations on the whole ship. Because of the water pressure outside the hull, it has to be done by means of compressed air. One mistake and the water pressure gets the best of the air pressure. Then disaster overwhelms the unfortunate operator. On the later submarines, however, this danger was removed by the installation of a septic tank, which is cleaned out when the ship surfaces.

Continuing to move aft through another bulkhead, you thread your way between giant diesel engines with their electric generators on either side, and then into the maneuvering room, in which are the electric motors that turn the propellers. On the surface their power comes from the generators attached to the diesels. The moment a submarine dives, electric controls shift the motors to the storage batteries and the engines are stopped. If this were not done, the diesels would quickly exhaust all the oxygen within the ship, and, more seriously, draw a vacuum which would cause eyes to pop out and eardrums to fracture. Aft of the maneuvering room there is a compartment of storage batteries and then the after-torpedo room, which is similar to the forward torpedo room but smaller. Here other members of the crew sleep soundly over huge amounts of TNT.

Incidentally, there are no steps in a submarine. Ladders go straight up and straight down. You climb from one deck to the next through a round hatchway which has a heavy, watertight cover.

The Navy has made every possible effort to compensate in different ways for the hard-line duty of the Submarine Service. For one thing, the submariners receive an augmented ration allowance, and without any doubt are the best fed sailors in the Navy. They get all the coffee they want whenever they want it. They're apt to call it Java or Joe. They can get a snack between meals if they want it. Many a submarine crew far out in the Pacific, away from their base for weeks, sit down to a meal that includes steak and strawberries. The Submarine Service has taken a leaf from the book of advice to brides—the way to a man's heart is through his stomach.

Every comfort which the limited space not occupied by machinery allows is provided for the men. Electric washing machines do away with elbow grease in laundering clothes. Unless attacking or under attack, the men very frequently are permitted to listen to the radio. (Mike Fenno let his crew hear Japanese propaganda broadcasts in English so they could see how ridiculous the Japanese were.) There are sun lamps for the men's health, so that submariners on long patrols look as if they had just returned from Miami Beach, rather than as if they had just crawled out from under a log. Reading matter, phonograph records, and games are available to the men off watch.

Probably the most important contribution to the comfort and health of the submariners is the air-conditioning equipment, especially since so much of our submarine fleet's patrolling during the war was in the humid tropics. Not only is air within our submarines kept at the right temperature, but all excess moisture is extracted. This moisture is then condensed and provides an average of about one hundred and fifty gallons of fresh water daily, or more than two gallons for each man aboard.

Best of all to a great many in the submarine crews, however, is the fact that a certain informality in wearing apparel is permitted. John Delmont Rogers, an electrician's mate second class, tells of a fellow crew member on a submarine who always wore a ten-gallon sombrero. Considering the headroom in a submarine, he must have been a short sailor. Another man, says Rogers, used to wear a little railroad fireman's cap. Whenever he went on watch, his first act was to sit down in the engine room, wave his long-visored cap and shout: "All aboard! Number 2 is ready to go!"

Footwear is likely to be even more curious than headgear. When a submarine is diving to escape a depth-charge attack, life itself may depend on absolute quiet on the part of the crew. Then hard-talking sailors go around whispering, everyone is careful not to bang into anything. The men on occasion take off their shoes and tiptoe about in stocking feet, or wear slippers, sneakers or sandals. Some of them have "go-aheads," consisting of a fiber or wooden sole and a single strap over the instep. Those with wooden soles are removed during attacks. If you go ahead in these contraptions, you're all right. If you back up, you're barefoot.

The reason for such extreme precautions is that the supersensitive listening devices used in warships today might well pick up even such a small sound as the scraping of an ordinary shoe, and reveal a hiding submarine's position. The Submarine Service demands that the men in it have pleasing personalities. They must be socially adjusted and able to get along with their fellows. A touchy disposition is out of place in the close quarters of a submarine.

The men must be prepared to endure cheerfully the monotony and routine of seemingly endless days on patrol. When not on watch, the crew members sometimes have difficulty finding enough diversion. They read, play cards, doze in their bunks; but any second they may be called on to spring to their battle stations, not knowing whether they are preparing to attack or are trying to avoid an attack by the enemy. The muffled explosion of depth charges is liable to give them the answer to that question.

When a depth bomb goes off underwater in the vicinity of a submarine, those aboard her hear a double report.

First comes the fairly sharp noise produced by the concussion, and close on top of it comes the rumbling blast of the explosion. Some idea of how close the depth charge was is obtained from this double report; the closer the bomb, the closer together the two sounds. What soldiers say of shells, submariners say of depth bombs: "It's the one you don't hear that gets you."

Life in a submarine in wartime is about the same for officers as for the enlisted men, except for their duties. In general, the third and fourth officers stand the periscope watches when the ship is submerged, and the "action watches" on the surface. The captain and the executive officer, as a rule, stand no regular watches. Perhaps it is more accurate to say that the captain stands a twenty-four-hour watch with the responsibility of the entire ship on his shoulders. He gets all the rest he can, but at night, especially while the submarine is running on the surface, he is likely to be awake or restless. The other three officers stand the diving watches at the diving controls when the ship is submerged, and the officer of the deck takes the watches on the surface.

A submarine's complement should be regarded as a single entity. The crew of a large bomber is often cited as an example of perfect coordination of effort: teamwork. But so long as the engines function, all the other members of a bomber crew from the tail gunner to the bombardier could be knocked out and the pilot might still fly the plane, bring it in and land it. Under parallel conditions in a submarine, the captain would be sunk—literally.

This feeling of the compactness and unity of every submarine crew was expressed by one of our commanders, who called the men under him together after he had been awarded the Navy Cross. He held up the medal so all could see it, and said, "There it is. I'll wear it, but it belongs to all of us."

The same idea, which is typical of the Submarine Service, was put into words by Lieutenant Commander Fenno. He said: "It's not any one man in a submarine who sinks an enemy ship. The captain may be a sort of matador who handles the kill, but it's the whole crew who have made it possible. Teamwork is absolutely essential. One little sailor in the stern can open a wrong valve and gum up the whole works, even bring disaster. If one man falls down, the whole plan of attack may be upset. In many ways it resembles the teamwork of a turret crew on a battleship. We don't have individual heroes in a submarine. When we win, we all win together. And if we go down, we all go down together."

The health of his crew is of primary concern to the captain, not only because there are so few facilities for taking care of sick men and only a pharmacist's mate to doctor them, but also because such things as colds may easily sweep through the entire personnel and lower the efficiency of the ship. When a man gets sick or is wounded or injured, a submarine can't go home, and is usually far away from a hospital ship. If a man dies, he's buried at sea.

As Mike Fenno pointed out, the decks of a submarine are always wet. He decided that most colds on his submarine were the result of wet feet, so each of his men was inspected before going on watch. Feet had to be well protected with rubbers or boots. Fenno also said that on his ship noses were counted every day, because a commander may not see every man in the crew, small as it is, oftener than once in three or four days when the submarine is on patrol.

It goes without saying that an excellent constitution is a must in the Submarine Service.

The modern submarine can, and often does, remain below surface for long periods of time. It can stay submerged for twenty-four hours without any difficulty; but twice that long was about the extreme limit of our submarines during the war. After V-E Day there were reports that the Germans had developed a U-boat which would remain underwater for more than a week and could travel as fast or faster submerged than on the surface. It would seem, however, that this high-speed submarine was still in the blueprint stage. Only the plans for it fell into our hands, and whether the completed ship could attain its hoped-for speed is problematical. Nevertheless, there is little doubt that such a development will come in time. Where do the men get the air to breathe? When a submarine dives, she takes it right down with her and that is all the air they have while submerged. Motors keep it in constant circulation.

Although carbon dioxide, generated in the lungs of the men who are breathing the air, is gradually added to the atmosphere, this doesn't make an important difference up to about a three percent concentration. After a day and a night submerged, though, it may reach a point at which the men are obliged to breathe more deeply, their judgment is liable to grow faulty, and they move with increasing difficulty. Before the air becomes this bad, a white powder known as carbon-dioxide absorbent is sprinkled around. It serves to purify the air to some extent. In dire emergencies, oxygen may be released from the tanks used to fill the Momsen escape lungs.

The Momsen lung is a device to enable men to escape from a sunken submarine. It is a form of oxygen mask, resembling a large hot-water bag, made of rubber and stockinet. When it is decided a submarine can't return to the surface, the ship's escape compartments are flooded, forming a large air pocket, or bubble, in each. In these pockets, the men don the escape lungs, which contain a can of soda lime to absorb the carbon dioxide in their breath. Then the Momsen lungs are filled with oxygen from tanks in the escape compartments. One by one, the men go out the escape hatch and, holding onto a line which has been sent to the surface so that their ascent will not be too rapid, they seek to rise to safety. They sometimes succeed.

Just how deep a submarine can go before the water caves it in is, quite naturally, a carefully guarded secret. However, the depth is more than four hundred feet, and the distance beneath the surface to which some of our undersea ships descended during war was almost unbelievable.

The Navy is not telling how far our submarines can travel submerged. This is a tricky question, anyway, since the submerged cruising range is in direct proportion to the speed at which the submarine travels. Occasionally a submariner will speak of a six-hour speed or a ten-hour speed, by which he means a rate of speed submerged that would exhaust the batteries in six hours or ten hours. A submarine moving at its top underwater speed will cover only about a tenth as much distance as it would at a very slow rate before it becomes necessary to surface and recharge batteries. By carefully nursing the supply of "juice," our new-type submarines easily negotiated more than a hundred miles submerged. On the other hand, it was possible to run the batteries down within a range of ten or fifteen miles, if an excessive load was put on them.

When submerged, it is essential for a submarine to keep moving, even though very slowly, in order to maintain trim. While it is not impossible for the ship to remain motionless underwater, suspended between the surface and the bottom, it is an operation that requires the highest skill and alertness on the part of the diving officer and hardly worth the trouble. By backing down on the surface, it also is possible to dive a submarine stern first. But again, hardly worth doing, except as a stunt.

The construction of a modern undersea craft is so sturdy that it can take any amount of pounding from the wind and waves, but in a heavy sea its limited freeboard is liable to make it appear to be running submerged, even though technically it is on the surface. As far as anyone knows, no submarine has ever capsized. There is a popular notion that once a submarine dives and has reached a certain depth, it encounters a sort of millpond calm and steadiness which enables it to cruise along on an even keel no matter how rough the sea overhead may be. This is only partially true. When the surface of the sea is choppy, even quite rough, a submarine can find still waters in the depths.

On the other hand, a long, deep groundswell, or the sweeping water movement that follows a heavy storm, will give an undersea craft a good rolling around, even at a considerable depth. A sailor needs stout sea legs at a time like that, and seasickness in the Submarine Service is not unknown.

If a submarine is too deep, or circumstances make it inadvisable to put up the periscope, the ship literally sees with its ears. Through her supersonic listening device—the sound gear—she not only determines her own movements but also keeps track of the movements of her target.

A submarine very often gets underwater ranges by means of "pinging," as the use of an echo-recording apparatus is called.

When a submarine under the surface wants to look at what is going on outside, it must use its eye—the periscope. The periscope is made of two steel tubes, one within the other. The inner one contains nitrogen under pressure, which keeps mist from obscuring the vision. In addition, the lenses have ray filters which improve the vision under different atmospheric conditions.

The importance of its periscope to a submarine is sharply emphasized by the fact that modern ships carry two of them, or rather two sets of them, since periscopes are of three kinds. These are the altiscope, night periscope, and attack periscope. The first enables the officer in the control room who is looking into the mirror at the periscope's base to obtain a view of the sky above, in order to spot airplanes. The night periscope is so designed that it gives the maximum transmission of light. The principal feature of the attack periscope is its small head, which reduces the chances of detection when the submarine is closing in on a target. Periscopes have different adjustments for the magnification of images, and they also have rangefinders. They are raised and lowered by electrically operated hoists.

The officer at the periscope—in an attack it is usually the submarine's commander—stands in the conning tower and looks into the eyepiece to see what is on the surface.

At the base of the periscope's steel cylinder two handles stick out; gripping these, the man at the periscope can turn it in any direction he desires. In front of him is the quartermaster at the steering wheel, called the helm, and usually behind him is the navigator with his charts. Nearby are push buttons for signaling to all parts of the submarine. The captain, or any other officer who may be at the periscope, is running the show and giving the commands.

Strictly speaking, a torpedo is not fired from a submarine, but is launched, since from the moment it emerges from the tube it is under its own power and becomes a self-propelled missile. A torpedo is started on its way by the compressed air in the torpedo tube. It is driven toward its destination by more compressed air, contained in a flask just behind its warhead at a pressure of some twenty-five hundred pounds per square inch.

Torpedoes of the type with which our submarines started the war have a standard diameter of twenty-one inches, although they vary in length. They are about twenty feet long, cylindrical in shape, and have a fairly blunt nose, a conical stern, and vertical and horizontal fins and rudders. There are three sections to a torpedo. Just behind the detonator, set in the nose, lies the warhead containing hundreds of pounds of TNT. Behind that is the compressed-air chamber, and then the so-called afterbody which contains depth-setting gear, gyro steering mechanism, and the twin turbines which turn two concentric propellers revolving in opposite directions. The turbines are driven by a mixture of alcohol and air which is converted into steam in a small but high-pressure boiler heated by a powerful burner. The afterbody is filled with a number of secret gadgets for controlling the course of the torpedo. Briefly, its depth is controlled by the horizontal rudder, which is operated by a small engine regulated, in turn, by hydrostatic pressure; and its lateral course is controlled by a gyrocompass, which operates the vertical rudder.

The speed at which this torpedo travels is adjustable. It can whiz along at more than forty knots with little difficulty and travel five miles or better. If a torpedo doesn't hit anything, it sinks at the end of its run. But this type of torpedo has one unfortunate weakness. As it travels through the water, it blazes a trail of bubbles—the torpedo track—which can easily be followed by the eye. When the war was less than two years old, however, the Navy managed to overcome this handicap by developing a wake-less torpedo, known as the Mark 18, which was especially effective for daylight attacks. Before the war against the Japanese ended, this new missile had accounted for some one million tons of enemy shipping, ranging from spitkits to the largest Japanese battleship. The first of these wake-less torpedoes was fired in September 1943; by July 1945, about thirty-two hundred of them had been launched in successful attacks, and there were plenty more in reserve.

The ten-thousandth Mark 18 came off the assembly line on V-J Day. Incidentally, the Germans also had developed and used a similar wake-less torpedo. The Mark 18 is driven by a special electric motor, weighing only a few pounds per horsepower. Power is supplied by a high-capacity storage battery. A filament-like wire in the battery compartment burns off the gases as they are generated. This weapon, which was built by the Western Electric Corporation at its Sharon, Pennsylvania, plant, was developed in the highest secrecy. The factory was surrounded by special guards and even use of the word "torpedo" was abandoned among the workmen.

It is very difficult to score a hit with any type of submarine torpedo unless the target is relatively close. In addition to aiming more than one hundred yards of steel submarine both horizontally and vertically, and adjusting the torpedo itself so that it will travel at the proper depth and speed and stay on its course, it is necessary to make careful calculations about the speed of the missile, the speed of the target, and the angle of the shot. Meanwhile, it is highly desirable, if not essential, to keep the attack concealed from the enemy. Usually the interval between the launching of the torpedo and the earliest moment it can hit its target is several minutes. With the old-type torpedo a quick-witted skipper had time to dodge the missile if he saw it coming. He often did. The cost of a torpedo is approximately ten thousand dollars. Each one takes up a great deal of room, and the number that even the biggest submarines can carry is strictly limited. This was one reason why submarine commanders were careful to use them only on worthwhile targets. Another reason was that torpedoes are not effective on vessels of very shallow draft—they're liable to run under them.

Although it was not without danger, because a submarine is vulnerable to gunfire, it was often more expedient to surface and use deck guns on small craft. The men on hard-line duty never hesitated to do this and save their torpedoes for another enemy ship.

Mitsubishi A6M Zero fighter on the aircraft carrier *Akagi*

4 – On Japan's Doorstep

As soon as Lieutenant Commander Fenno brought the submarine *Trout* back to Pearl Harbor after delivering the gold to the mainland, the officers and men were sent ashore for rest and relaxation, while a relief crew took over the overhauling and refitting of their ship. Fenno and his men had earned a holiday. During the preceding eighty-three days, since they started out on patrol shortly before the outbreak of war, they had been at sea all but three days!

From January 1, 1942, until the middle of June, the *Trout* was in port only eighteen days altogether. In those early months of the war, our hard-hitting submarines were hardly given time to catch their breath; they were kept at sea, holding the line against the powerful Japanese Navy, while we struggled desperately to build up our own shattered sea power.

In speaking of the operations of our submarines in the Pacific, Mike Fenno remarked: "You really go out there! Way out there!" When he appeared at Admiral Withers' Flag Office to receive the orders for his third wartime patrol, he learned that he was indeed to go way, way out there—some thirty-five hundred miles straight across the Pacific Ocean to the coast of Japan. After the Admiral had given Fenno his orders, he said: "Get on your horse! I'll be glad to see you back!"

Fenno wasted no time in shoving off on the long haul. It was the middle of March. There had been some changes in the officers aboard the American submarine. Pitts had left and gone to Submarine School. Harlfinger had been transferred to new construction, where he was to watch the step-by-step building of a new ship on which he later would return to the Pacific. In their places were Ensign David Gaston and Ensign Ray Ulman.

Day after day the *Trout* followed the sun toward Japan. She made good time, driving forward on the surface except for occasional practice dives. But there was a monotonous sameness about each day, with little to make one different from another beyond variations in the weather, none of the excitement and suspense of hunting in enemy waters.

The lack of action irked Dave Gaston particularly. He was from Los Angeles and had been captain-elect of the UCLA football team until he entered the Navy, full of drive and itching to have a chance at the Japanese. Stationed on a tender at San Diego, he managed to transfer to the submarines and landed in Fenno's craft under instruction assigned to the gunnery officer. Gaston made no effort to conceal his disappointment at the lack of activity as the hours rolled by. Again and again, he lamented that he hadn't joined some branch of the service in which he could really come to grips with the Japanese.

A week went by, and Japan was still far away. The *Trout* ran into heavy weather, and it was while George Schottler, ever ready with a wisecrack, was on watch that Fenno called up to him and asked:

"Is it calming down, George?" At that instant a huge wave rolled over the bridge and soaked Schottler. Spluttering, he shouted back: "Yes, sir! But look out—it's calmin' right down the hatch!"

More tedious days, with nothing to see ahead but mile after mile of Pacific Ocean and nothing to see astern but the same thing, boiling with their own wake. At last they reached the Bonins, the heavily fortified island outposts of Japan corresponding in some degree to our own Hawaiian Islands. But the *Trout* slipped past the enemy's sea bastion without being detected.

Then came the time when Mike Fenno's big gray submarine really arrived "way out there." Through the haze on the horizon could be seen the dim smudge that was the Land of the Rising Sun. The submarine worked her way closer and closer to Honshu, largest of the Japanese home islands, until she was almost on the doorstep of Kobe and Osaka.

For a couple of days, Fenno reconnoitered the coast around the entrance to Osaka Bay. Then, while his ship was lying submerged only about half a mile off the beach, along came two freighters from the direction of Tokyo. The *Trout* promptly took after them and fired four torpedoes. Fenno described it sadly. "All four missed." It was an inauspicious beginning, but the crew refused to be downhearted. Instead, they organized a pool on the Japanese ships they intended to sink. The clock was divided into twenty-three-minute sections. One section was assigned to each of the twenty men in the pool. If a ship was sunk within your three minutes of any hour—you won the jackpot!

The next day a coal burning freighter hove over the horizon and plodded along toward the waiting submarine. "Down comes this 'smoker' about a mile off the beach," Fenno said. "She's between us and the mainland. A good setup."

Bad luck still dogged the Americans. They let go a torpedo at the target, but there was no triumphant explosion. Fenno raised the periscope.

"She's running down the coast," he said. "We let her have another torpedo, but that missed too. Then out from behind the smoker pops a patrol boat. She must have been using the other ship as a screen.

"They'd evidently located us from the torpedo track because they both came toward us bow on. We dove and got out of the way. I was pretty down in the mouth. Six torpedoes fired—and nothing hit. I told myself, 'That's the worst you've ever done'."

That night the American submarine moved out to sea to charge her batteries. Gloom was thick inside her round hull. And the next day was so foggy she couldn't get back to resume her hunting. Meanwhile, however, Fenno analyzed the situation and when he headed his craft toward the mainland the following morning he believed he had the answer. The submarine slipped well up into the bay. She was almost in sight of Kobe, one of Japan's major cities.

"Early in the afternoon, we were lying a couple of miles off the beach," Fenno said. "About three miles farther up the bay, on a point, was a big fort. On the shore we could see a long row of nice new barracks. They stretched almost up to the fort. We also could make out some shore batteries.

"Along came a tanker. She was headed just outside of us. I waited until she was good and close—and then we poked her with two stern torpedoes!"

The twin explosions that followed blew all the gloom right out of the submarine. Twice hit, the mortally wounded tanker swung toward the beach. Fenno took a look around through the periscope and spied a freighter coming up. She too swung toward the beach, apparently intent on helping the sinking tanker. Suddenly, however, the cargo ship realized that the tanker had been torpedoed, and again changed her course.

"I fired a torpedo at the freighter," Fenno said. "No luck."

Once more the freighter swung and started to run for the beach. Then things began to happen fast. The man at the sound gear reported that he had picked up a fast-moving propeller. Quickly the submarine's periscope swept around, and Fenno spotted the bridge of a destroyer coming in behind them. "That was one of the hardest decisions I ever made in my life," he said. "But I decided to ignore the destroyer. I didn't look at it again. We closed in on that tanker and freighter.

"By this time the tanker was about five hundred yards off the beach and sinking fast. The freighter was five hundred yards behind the tanker. They were badly rattled on board her, because once more they tried to swing out away from the beach. "She was a perfect target. We poked a torpedo right in her belly. We got both those ships."

For the moment, the *Trout* had just about cleared the area of Japanese shipping. For some unexplained reason the destroyer failed to enter the fight. Whether she was afraid she might intercept one of the American torpedoes that were churning up the sea, and chose to save her face by turning it away, or whether those aboard, hypnotized by their own overconfidence, simply couldn't believe that a Yankee submarine was operating so close to Japan are questions that never will be answered. The shore batteries and big guns of the fort, for which the submarine would have been within easy range, remained silent, strangely enough. Perhaps the Japanese who manned them also couldn't believe their eyes.

The men in the submarine were puzzled but grateful. The immediate area, however, was not safe to linger in and the *Trout* cleared it as fast as possible. Fenno didn't go far, though; he had found a good hunting ground. He slipped the submarine out to sea and recharged her batteries. When the *Trout* came back in, she moved even farther up the bay than before, in defiance of the fort on the point. There she lay in wait.

A couple of days passed before a likely target appeared, but when it did, it was a good one—a big freighter of about fifteen thousand tons coming in.

"We closed in a little and waited for her to cross our bow," Fenno said, describing the attack. "Just as the range started to increase, we fired one torpedo. It missed, so we let her have a second. That one hit under her bottom, and it made a terrific racket." To explode a torpedo under the bottom of an enemy vessel is a bull's-eye for a submarine because the chances are that it will break the craft's back. This time, however, the target managed to hold together and run for the beach. The *Trout*, periscope down, took after her.

"I figured on waiting for ten minutes before looking, but I got impatient and put the periscope up after six minutes," Fenno admitted. "That darned freighter was still going! So we fired a third torpedo at her, but she managed to dodge it."

The submarine chased the big cargo ship right up under the guns of the fort, like a terrier chasing a hog under a barn. The attack, however, convinced the Japanese of the presence of the American undersea ship and made the area definitely hot. Not only was the *Trout* well within point-blank range of the fort, but the Japanese antisubmarine patrol was starting to buzz around her like angry bees. The Americans got out of there fast.

"The last view I had of that big Jap freighter," Fenno said, "she was sinking low by the stern. I feel sure she went down, but we didn't claim that one, because we didn't actually see her sink."

At this stage of the game the Japanese were two, and probably three, down to the Americans. And although the enemy knew they were somewhere around, and the anti-submarine patrol was growing thicker, Fenno and his men continued to prowl that part of Tokyo's ocean, hunting enemy shipping. The Japanese, however, were liberal with their depth bombs and laid down patterns all over the area in which they imagined the submarine was hiding. Sometimes she was. The torpedo attacks by the submarine and the depth-charge attacks against her had by this time completely converted Dave Gaston. Lounging in the wardroom one day, he announced:

"Just think. Two months ago, I was sittin' in San Diego. Wait'll I get back to the tender, and I'll tell those boys!"

Eventually, Gaston did get back to the tender, and the boys gave him a luncheon at which he was scheduled to unlimber his tall tales about life in a submarine in the war zone. But before he had a chance to tell them, there was an air-raid alert. Everyone present, except Dave, ran from the table to take his station. Gaston was left alone—without an audience.

The thrill of submarine warfare so completely captivated the one-time skeptic that he reached a point where he described diving in a submarine as, "just like pulling the blankets over your head and lying down in your bunk to sleep."

The area at the entrance to Osaka Bay was given a chance to cool off a little, while the *Trout* undertook another mission—a futile hunt for a reported Japanese carrier. Again slipping through the Bonins without detection, she moved on to the coast of Honshu and well up into the bay, which had proved her best hunting ground. With her screws barely turning, so that the five-knot current carried her backward a knot or so, she lurked around the point that was guarded by the Japanese fort.

Before long two ships appeared, outward bound. One was a freighter and the other was a fair-sized naval auxiliary, without a sign of an escort.

"We had only one torpedo left in our bow tubes, but we got a beautiful shot at the larger ship, the auxiliary. It didn't do us much good. She saw the track of the torpedo in time to dodge it.

"She swung and started to run. We swung the other way in order to bring our stern tubes to bear. Just at that moment, the smaller ship came blundering across our stern." Fenno's eyes sparkled as he told it. "We poked her with two torpedoes, and she simply fell apart!"

Meanwhile, a third Japanese ship had come along. When she discovered what was going on, she turned and joined the auxiliary in a scramble to get away. The submarine took up the chase, but after a few minutes Fenno saw that they couldn't catch the two fleeing vessels, so gave it up and cleared the area.

The *Trout* had been raising hob in the enemy's front yard for three weeks all told. She had been hanging around the fortified point so long that the crew had begun to call it Fenno Point. The Japanese were extremely annoyed; they increased the antisubmarine defense till the patrol boats were thick as ants at a picnic. Each evening at sundown, as many as a hundred boats would come out, hoping to catch the submarine when she surfaced to charge her batteries. They were all types and sizes. Sampans, fishing boats, and other spitkits, as Navy men call small nondescript craft, as well as a sprinkling of destroyers.

But Fenno's submarine still had time, torpedoes, fuel and food. She refused to be frightened off. One night in the control room, several of the crew were holding a bull session and telling what messages they'd like to have come over the radio. The last to announce his choice was Maurice ("Doc") McConnell, the pharmacist's mate. That "Doc" was more than a nickname; on a submarine a pharmacist's mate is all the doctor they have, and he supplies the needed pills for aches and pains, as well as first aid for injuries.

"The message I'd like to get," Doc drawled, "is this: 'Dear Submarine—Please come home. Love and kisses—The Admiral'."

That's the way it was in the submarines on long patrols in distant waters. As the time to head for home drew near, the crews began to grow restless, to hanker for Honolulu, or whatever base they were operating from. Yet after the men had been ashore a few days, they started to show the same signs of eagerness to get back on patrol, even though they had hardly had time to rest after the last trip into enemy seas.

The *Trout*, however, still had work to do, and since the Admiral wasn't likely to summon her home with love and kisses before her task was accomplished, she set about it. Fenno himself was far from satisfied with what he had accomplished, and even though the members of the crew thought longingly of the delights of Oahu, they were equally anxious to chalk up a few more Japanese ships.

There's something about submarines that gets in a man's blood. Cases in which submarine men ask to be transferred to other branches are extremely rare, and this could hardly be laid to the extra pay alone. Possibly it's the hunting instinct. Your sportsman hunter will go to endless expense, trouble and hardship to bring back a brace of ducks, a pheasant or a deer. He'll travel to distant places, risk fevers and journey through steaming jungles so that he can come home and boast he has shot an elephant. But all other hunting shrinks into triviality beside hunting in deadly, modern submarines, with the game anything from a spitkit to a mighty battleship.

The *Trout*'s next victory was an easy one. The night was moonless, but bright with starlight. The submarine was on the surface, charging her batteries.

"We spotted a patrol boat ... a good-sized ship," Fenno said. "Still on the surface, we moved toward the Jap. He saw us, swung and headed our way. We dove and kept an eye on him through the periscope.

"As soon as he came close enough, we let him have a torpedo. It slammed right into him."

The submarine waited underwater for a few minutes, meanwhile maneuvering back to her original position. When she pushed her dripping bow through the surface again, the stars were still shining brightly overhead. All around lay the shimmering sea, but there was no Japanese patrol boat to mar the beauty of the night.

"I never worried about that one," Fenno said. "He sank fast!"

For a few more days, the Americans ranged up and down the Japanese coast without getting a chance at an enemy ship. This didn't suit the aggressive captain who, contemptuous of the antisubmarine patrol, headed his ship right back to the hunting ground off "Fenno Point." It was calm as the proverbial millpond, but the visibility was low because of a foggy haze, so the *Trout* moved into the area on the surface. It was late in the morning before she dove.

Then came a few hours of patient waiting. In a submarine stalking enemy shipping patience is more than a virtue, it's an essential to success. About one o'clock in the afternoon, the perseverance of the Americans was rewarded. Down came a freighter, approaching at an angle. This was to be the big Yankee submarine's farewell to Japan on this patrol; she had only two torpedoes left. Both were in the stern tubes, so she turned her back toward the Japanese for her parting shots.

The first torpedo missed the target, but the second slammed into the cargo ship with an explosion that brought cheers from the weary submarine men and tore a gaping hole in the enemy.

Fenno smacked his lips with satisfaction as he recalled it. "We just waited and watched that baby sink!" For twenty-eight days the rugged *Trout* had been ripping into enemy shipping against the background of Japan's beaches and defenses, only a few miles from two of her principal cities. Now the submarine's torpedoes were gone.

The men who had never faltered through the tense, nerve-racking hours, with death always near, were triumphant but weary. When the last torpedo had found its mark and the American submarine was lying deep beneath the ocean, Fenno turned to Al Clark.

"Let's go home," he said. Mike Fenno, while he was growing up in Westminster, Massachusetts, attended Fitchburg High School, where he laid the groundwork for the baseball ability that put him on the Naval Academy baseball team for three years. He also was assistant varsity baseball coach at the Academy in 1933 and coach in 1934-35. It was at Fitchburg High that he received his nickname.

"They were mostly Irish there," he explains. "I guess Fenno sounded sort of Italian to them, so they made me an Irishman with a nickname."

From tossing a baseball around a diamond to pitching torpedoes into Japanese ships is a long throw. But Fenno's submarine had run up a good score on the enemy's home grounds. Out of twelve attacks she had sunk six enemy vessels, although only five were claimed, because no one aboard actually saw the big freighter go down under the guns of the fort.

"We should have got them all," Fenno said regretfully as he recounted the toll. In spite of his baseball years, Mike Fenno seemed to have forgotten that they never yet have sent anyone who was batting .500 back to the minor leagues. Next came the Battle of Midway. The *Trout* was on patrol in the general area in which this smashing American naval victory was achieved, but no enemy ship encroached on her immediate section and she had no chance to take an active part.

In this tremendous and crucial sea fight, in which neither of the fleets engaged saw the other, but relied entirely on their air arms, the submarine watched plenty of planes, both our own and those of the enemy, wing overhead as she cruised about in the vain hope of planting some torpedoes in Japanese warcraft. A day or so after the battle, however, Fenno received orders to investigate a lot of wreckage and debris which had been spotted in the midst of a large oil slick. The slick was located by the submarine without much trouble, and she started into it. On the bridge were men armed with a tommy gun and two machine guns. The officer of the deck had a businesslike forty-five strapped to his waist. The captain was taking no chances.

They began picking up pieces of debris which were easily identified by their markings as Japanese. There was no doubt that something disastrous had taken place. Cautiously the *Trout* picked her way farther into the slick, gathering more and more evidence of a Japanese catastrophe. Then one of the lookouts called attention to what seemed to be a large ball fender such as ships use. The submarine swung toward it and slowly moved ahead. Topside, everyone was alert, with the entire assortment of weapons trained on the strange object.

"Our bow was almost up to it," Fenno said, "when up jumped a couple of men. They were two Jap sailors. They'd been sitting on a raft which was just under the surface, and had pulled a blanket over their heads when they sighted us. I couldn't help thinking at the time that the scene was kind of ridiculous. All those guns trained on two shipwrecked and wobbly Japs—they were so weak and emaciated they could hardly stand."

The two Japanese were hauled aboard the submarine. Originally there had been twenty men on the raft, but these two were the only survivors after four days adrift. Gaston picked them up one at a time and carried them below on his shoulder like sacks of meal. They were laid on a couple of mattresses placed on the deck up forward and turned over to the ministrations of Doc McConnell. Half-starved and terrified sailors of the Japanese Navy were something new for Doc, but that didn't cramp his style. First, he offered them each a shot of whisky. Apparently afraid to refuse it, they gulped it down. The results were terrible, as the Japanese were not only unfed but also unused to such liquids. The whisky bounced right up again.

"That really scared them," Fenno said. "It must have burned a little as it went down, and I guess they thought we were trying to poison them."

Doc held a consultation with the members of the crew who were looking on and the diagnosis was that the prisoners needed food rather than drink.

But their first meal was no more successful than their first drink. With mistaken generosity the Japanese were given large quantities of food; they couldn't hold it any better than the drinks.

Doc persisted, however, and starting with a liquid diet, eventually brought the two men back to health and strength. After a while they became very enthusiastic about the fine rations for our submarine crews. Toward the end of the patrol, the prisoners were allowed to clean up the mess and they had an opportunity to eat as much as they wanted. Life had never been like that in Japan.

The two prisoners were left in Doc's hands for medical attention after their capture and to members of the crew for guarding. One of them was small, thin and cheerful; the crew promptly named him "Pinhead." The other, who was bigger and inclined to be surly, was called "Fatso." With adroit questioning Pinhead and Fatso yielded much valuable information, some of which helped the Navy in piecing together the picture of the Midway victory.

Directed by Fenno, Doc McConnell learned from them that they were from a cruiser of the 8,500-ton Mogami class, one of Tokyo's formidable types of cruisers.

Their ship had been sunk. They also disclosed that the *Mogami* herself had been sent to the bottom, as well as a destroyer in their formation. They may have realized that this and other information they revealed would be useful to the United States, but it didn't stop them from talking.

The two prisoners were a source of constant amusement and interest to the members of the crew, who deluged them with attention. They were blindfolded, so they couldn't see any of the secret details of the submarine, and were led to the showers. They were given candy bars, apparently something the Japanese didn't get very often, for they hugged their presents ecstatically. They also got new clothes. When picked up they had been wearing only ragged, water-soaked coveralls, but when they left the ship at Pearl Harbor for internment, the sailors of Fenno's submarine supplied them with dungarees, shoes and other items of clothing. And in the Navy the enlisted men buy their own clothes after the initial allowance is expended.

The crew's relations with the prisoners, and especially Doc McConnell's questioning of them, were made all the more interesting by the fact that nobody aboard the submarine could speak Japanese and Pinhead and Fatso couldn't speak any English. Well, hardly any, that is ... Some of the members of the crew showed them pictures in movie magazines. At the sight of a famous American star, their eyes brightened, and they became articulate enough to exclaim:

"Ho, Cluck! Cluck Gable!"

Another well-known performer's likeness brought forth delighted squeals from the two Japs, and the cry:

"Mickey Moose! Mickey Moose!"

As for George Raft, when they were shown his picture they squinted their eyes to slits, closed their hands with one finger extended to simulate a gun, and shouted: "Ah! Boom-boom! Boom-boom!"

Mice and gangsters. That was about as far as the ordinary Japanese had gone toward an appreciation of what constituted the American way of life.

The original *Mogami* in July 1935, shortly after commissioning

5 – Adventure in the Spice Islands

WHEN THE WAR STARTED, Lieutenant Theodore C. Aylward's submarine was one of a number stationed in the Philippines and operating out of Manila. Aylward's ship was the *Sea Raven*, one of the four submarines that comprised Division 17, a veteran unit on the Asiatic Station.

Our modern undersea craft have been named for various fishes or, in a few cases, other aquatic inhabitants. And despite the name, a *Sea Raven* is not a bird, but a fish—a sculpin of the North Atlantic coast of America. Division 17, as a matter of fact, offered what sounded like the nucleus of a seagoing menagerie. Besides the *Sea Raven*, the other ships in it were the *Sea Lion*, which came to an inglorious end early in the war, the *Sea Dragon* and the *Sea Wolf*. It was a tough and rugged outfit, and the division's song, which was sung to the tune of "Solomon Levy," proclaimed it proudly. This ditty, which had countless verses, began:

> *Uncle cuts up sewer pipes and shapes them into boats,*
> *And sends them out to China, that's assuming that they floats;*
> *But of all the built and building, the finest ever seen*
> *Were the fighting undersea craft of Division 17.*

This was no idle boast. The *Sea Raven* and the *Sea Wolf* made records during the war that definitely put them among the finest ever seen.

The Aylward ship was a fleet submarine, large and relatively new. Her displacement on the surface was 1,450 tons, her length 310 feet, and she carried a normal complement of 55 officers and men. She cost about $5,500,000 to build.

At the moment when the Japanese opened their attack on the United States, the *Sea Raven* was anchored off the navy yard at Cavite, on Manila Bay. Her quartermaster had made a deal with a Chinese to get some special charts, which were to be delivered on December 8. The submarine was waiting for them, but the Japanese arrived with bombs before the Chinese could arrive with charts.

After dark on December 9, the submarine shoved off and she anchored at Mariveles, just outside the bay, about three o'clock the next afternoon. Her captain was eager to come out of his corner and start punching Japanese, but again he waited until dark before getting underway and passing through the minefields to the open sea. Once clear of the minefields that night, Aylward pointed the *Sea Raven* toward her first area of wartime patrol—off the northwest corner of Formosa. The war was two days old.

Aylward's submarine, however, had been in this same general area only a few weeks before, at the end of November, on what might be called a semi-wartime mission, a curtain raiser for the big show.

She had been one of four American submarines sent out to pick up the liner *President Harrison*, evacuating American nationals and Marines from China, and to act as an escort. She ran into a storm which Aylward said was beyond question the worst one he ever encountered in all his years at sea. (He graduated from the Naval Academy in 1926.) As a result, the submarine was half a day late for her rendezvous, but nevertheless managed to make a contact with the *Harrison* and escorted her into Olongapo, on Subic Bay, in the Philippines. That was more than the other three submarines in the division accomplished. Because of the storm, they never did pick up the *Harrison*.

On that mission, Aylward discovered that the area off Hoka Sho Light, north of Formosa, was "lousy with patrol boats." While Saburo Kurusu and Ambassador Nomura were conducting their "peace talks" with Secretary Hull in Washington, the Japanese were marshaling their anti-submarine patrol, knowing well that the American undersea fleet would start after them the instant their treachery, was exposed, and would strike hard and fast. Whatever information Tokyo may have had about the rest of our fleet before the Pearl Harbor attack, the Nipponese warlords must have been informed by their spies that our submarines, at least, were ready.

Grimly, the American warship drove northward toward Formosa. Aside from the tenseness and controlled excitement of the first days of war, life in Aylward's craft was uneventful during the early part of the voyage. But as she reached the area of her patrol, she again ran into a violent storm. For several days, she took a good bouncing around, but she rode it out unharmed and on Christmas Eve began prowling Formosan waters.

On Christmas Day, dinner was eaten before daylight, at an early hour even for breakfast. On war patrol, the hearty meal of the day always is breakfast. It can be prepared while the submarine is still on the surface and protected by darkness. Then, the cooking is limited only by the skill and mood of the cook, and the ventilating system will expel any attendant grease, smoke and odors. When the ship is submerged, cooking obviously must be kept to a minimum.

Aboard Aylward's submarine that Christmas Day there was turkey and cranberry sauce, fresh vegetables, pie and trimmings. If anything, the meal was merely spiced by the thought that momentarily a Japanese destroyer or bomber might come ripping through the darkness to interrupt their festivities with an alarm for battle stations.

There was a Christmas tree too—the control panel by that name in the control room, with its many red and green lights.

Some of the men aboard had Christmas boxes sent long before. The skipper was one of them. When Aylward was transferred from Pearl Harbor to the Philippine Station, his wife remained in Honolulu.

"Early in December, before war broke out," he said, "I received a Christmas package from her. It had a big sticker on it, warning me not to open it until Christmas.

"There we were—patrolling off Formosa. And there was my present all nicely wrapped up. I tore off the seals and tissue paper, opened the box. Well, it was a grand Christmas gift—three pairs of beautiful silk pajamas." He laughed. "They were all labeled 'Made in Japan'!"

But pajamas weren't the only Japanese-made objects in those parts that day. Later in the morning, the alarm for battle stations sounded through the submarine. The men hurried to their posts; some clamped on the earphones of the battle telephone system, others stood by, alert and tense.

At the eyepiece of the periscope, in the control room, Aylward studied the horizon carefully. Slowly growing larger in the lens was the outline of an enemy cargo ship.

In low crisp tones the skipper passed the order to make ready two torpedo tubes. Presently, the chief of the boat reported:

"Torpedoes ready, sir."

This was the first enemy ship the *Sea Raven* had encountered.

"She was a long way off," Aylward said, "and we didn't have a chance of closing in. Nevertheless, we let her have one torpedo."

He paused and ran a meditative forefinger over his neatly clipped mustache. Finally he said slowly:

"That one got away."

It was the only enemy cargo ship Aylward's submarine saw in the area. Christmas afternoon, however, she sighted a lot of sailing vessels. There were big ones, there were little ones. No matter how she tried, the submarine was unable to get rid of them, and that night when she surfaced flares appeared in all directions. The Japanese radio often complained about our submarines surfacing and shooting up "harmless" fishing boats and other small sailing craft.

Harmless? Our submarine commanders didn't think so. There was nothing harmless about the two-way radios they carried to summon bombers and destroyers. There was nothing harmless about their machine guns or the depth bombs some of them had on deck. After seven fruitless days off Formosa, Aylward received orders to return to the Philippines. The Japanese were reported preparing to land troops at Subic Bay in an attempt to outflank General MacArthur's forces on Bataan Peninsula, and Aylward's mission was to patrol off the bay and try to break up the landings. When she reached the area, however, the American submarine failed to sight any enemy transports. It was not until sometime later that the Japanese actually went ashore at Subic.

Aylward and his crew had their New Year's celebration off Subic. It was a nice night for it. As the submarine cruised along the surface, her big diesels charging her batteries, a full moon spread its glow over the waters rolling and tumbling on all sides. The moon was astern, and in that direction the visibility was excellent. Ahead, however, a haze hanging close to the surface restricted the range of vision.

The *Sea Raven* was in waters which the enemy's ships dominated and ranged over with impunity. The Japanese had only our insufficient air and submarine forces to worry about. It was not much of a surprise, therefore, to the officers and men topside when out of the murk ahead a couple of destroyers suddenly began to take shape. For a minute or two the Americans imagined that this was just the opportunity they had been hoping for. The enemy quickly changed their minds. Both destroyers pointed straight for the submarine, silhouetted against the moonlight.

In a submarine, caution is better than bravado. A good commander is a firm believer in the philosophy that has been expressed down through the ages: "He who flees will fight again." Submarines are not built to slug toe to toe with enemy warships; their purpose is to get in—and then get out. Aylward got out, and fast. "We made a quick dive," he said. "There was no doubt the Japs had seen us before we spotted them."

The New Year's party was on. A pattern of depth bombs in a lonely stretch of ocean makes more noise than a battery of tin horns in Times Square, but it isn't so much fun.

"We dove in 1941—and surfaced in 1942," Aylward said.

"That annoyed the crew. Being forced to stay down while the New Year was coming in. Most of the resolutions they made, I'm certain, were concerned with what we would do to the Japs in retaliation."

Down along the west coast of the Philippines to Zamboanga, on Mindanao Island, the *Sea Raven* continued her patrol without encountering any more enemy craft, either war or cargo. As she passed through the swift and treacherous waters of Basilan Strait, however, she ran into an eerie and mysterious experience.

It was in the dead of night; the submarine was fighting the six- or seven-knot current on the surface. High overhead, a number of emergency flares suddenly lit up. Aboard the submarine, recognition signals were promptly given. Nothing happened. Again, the submarine attempted to identify herself and get a response. Still no answer, nor were there any more emergency flares. Completely puzzled, the skipper finally pulled his ship away from the area.

"We never learned what they meant," Aylward commented. "The most likely explanation we could figure out was that they came from a plane of the Philippine Scouts. For some reason, they couldn't answer our recognition signals. Either they didn't know them, or it was too late."

The American submarine moved over to Davao, where the Japanese by this time had landed and were fast spreading out. But before the Aylward submarine could get in any blows at the Nipponese shipping she was ordered to proceed to Port Darwin, Australia.

Her course took her down through Molucca Passage and past the Celebes Islands. The voyage was uneventful except for the crossing of the equator; as usual, the crew held the traditional Neptune ceremony to initiate those members who never before had been below the imaginary line. But those aboard, as their first wartime patrol drew near its close, were forced to suffer one of the most distressing hardships that could befall them—they ran out of cigarettes.

"They tried everything," Aylward said. "Some of the men rolled cigarettes out of coffee flavored with vanilla. I understand it was terrible. A few of them even puffed on chopped-up plug chewing tobacco. None of the ersatz was satisfactory."

At Port Darwin, the *Sea Raven* received an overhaul and was refitted. The members of her crew stretched their legs ashore and got a little rest and relaxation. Eight days later they shoved off on their second wartime patrol. Camranh Bay on the bulge of what had formerly been French Indo-China is one of the finest harbors in the world, and the Japanese, having seized it, were utilizing its facilities to the fullest in their sprawling sweep to overrun the East Indies. Aylward was ordered to patrol off Camranh.

His course led him up past Timor and Amboina and through the Moluccas. These are the fabulous and romantic Spice Islands of the swashbuckling navigators of the sixteenth and seventeenth centuries. They are scattered over a wide stretch of ocean between the Celebes and New Guinea, and include such relatively large islands as Halmahera, Ceram, Boroe and Aroe. The Spice Islands were discovered in 1512 by the Portuguese, who gave them their descriptive name. A century later aggressive Dutch traders and adventurers took them over and secured a monopoly on the clove trade. The British, coveting these rich possessions, twice gained a foothold there. The stubborn Dutch, however, not only managed to oust the intruders, but by the early part of the nineteenth century had solidified their claim to the islands and the spices. It remained undisputed until the coming of the Japanese.

"It's easy to understand why the early explorers called the Moluccas the Spice Islands," Aylward said. "The air was so balmy and fragrant, and it was just so darned nice that we hated to dive."

The reluctance of those aboard the *Sea Raven* to submerge and leave the spice-laden air was a complete change from the usual attitude of submarine crews in wartime. In peace, to be sure, they always have preferred to cruise on the surface, but when the dangers of antisubmarine patrol both on the sea and in the air surrounded them, they discovered there was something reassuring and restful in the ocean's depths.

In the Spice Islands, on the other hand, even a deep dive gives a submarine no assurance that it is hidden from enemy eyes. The area has some of the clearest water to be found in any of the seven seas, and by night it is unusually phosphorescent. These conditions don't contribute to the peace of mind of submarine crews.

"The Dutch fliers out there claimed they could see a submarine two hundred feet beneath the surface," Aylward said.

Through this aromatic paradise the submarine worked her way northward until she was moving through the Molucca Passage. Then came a beautiful calm night with a full moon to give high visibility and add to the natural loveliness of the scene, as the submarine pushed ahead on the surface.

"It was almost as bright as day," Aylward said. "The lookout was a quartermaster second named Kelly. Or, rather, he was a lad who wasn't named Kelly. He had an Italian name—Anastasia—but after war started, the chief of the boat told him, 'From now on your name is Kelly!' And from then on it was.

"This Kelly had only ordinary eyesight in the daytime, but at night he had eyes like a cat. In fact, he was known on the submarine as Cat Eyes. I never knew a better night lookout. Anyway, Kelly spotted the masts of a destroyer at about twelve thousand yards. And that's seeing 'em."

Submerged submarine attacks at night are the exception rather than the rule, but the big moon was flooding the area with light, so there was nothing for the *Sea Raven* to do but make an underwater approach.

"We dove and began to close in," Aylward said. "The Jap was on a zigzag, but we finally got her lined up. She was making about eighteen knots. We fired two torpedoes. The first one missed; the second hit her at the stern. There was a nice explosion. "It apparently put the destroyer out of control because she started to make a big circle. She shot across our bow and then looped around. Just as she came astern of us, there was a series of small explosions aboard her. That finished her up. A few minutes later, she sank."

Sinking that ship was a pretty satisfying achievement to the men aboard the submarine, particularly because the victim had been one of the enemy's large new-type destroyers—and a warship is bigger game than a freighter. Aylward's submarine, in hanging up her first scalp of the war, had got one with long hair. The next ship the *Sea Raven* sighted was at the east end of Sibutu Pass, which is about eighteen miles long. This was a large merchant vessel, but because of the strong adverse currents the American submarine was unable to get close enough for a torpedo shot. All through the Netherlands East Indies, the currents, which range from three to as high as nine knots, were a frequent source of trouble to underwater craft.

The Americans pressed on through the Sulu Sea without encountering any enemy shipping. They passed Palawan, the westernmost of the Philippine Islands, and emerged into the South China Sea in the vicinity of what is known as the "dangerous ground." This is a large area filled with reefs and hidden rocks, entirely uncharted. On all charts appears the warning to mariners to avoid it. It is exactly what its name indicates. The *Sea Raven* skirted the southern edge of this area, rounded it and headed north. And then she ran head on into a Japanese fleet. It was just before dark and difficult to see far, so the submarine was only about six thousand yards away when she spotted the enemy warships. The Nipponese force consisted of four cruisers and eight destroyers—a nice group of targets for a submarine with plenty of torpedoes aboard. But, on the other hand, eight destroyers carry a lot of depth bombs.

"It was good and rough," Aylward said, "and we managed to sneak in until we were only about fifteen hundred yards from one of the cruisers. She was a perfect setup. I told myself that this time we couldn't miss. We fired four torpedoes—and we did miss! With all four of them. That was one of the biggest disappointments of my life."

The Americans' tough luck had not ended, either.

"When we fired the torpedoes," Aylward continued, "we lost depth control and broached. Those Japs came right after us, and in no time at all we had eight destroyers bearing down on us at full speed."

The *Sea Raven* made a quick dive that was extra quick. The "dangerous ground" she had just avoided was nothing compared to the danger she now found herself in. Depth bombs began to churn up a wide area of the South China Sea, as the Japanese laid down their charges with zeal, if not effectiveness. They were persistent too. For eight hours the submarine stayed down and when she finally surfaced she could still hear the Nipponese on her listening device, although she couldn't see them. Enough was enough. She continued on her course toward Hainan.

After patrolling the area around Hainan for a number of days, without sighting a thing, the *Sea Raven* was ordered back to the Java Sea. This time she passed to the north of the "dangerous ground" and down by Corregidor. On the voyage south she spotted another submarine and, fearing it might be Japanese, refrained from using recognition signals. The other underwater craft, apparently, believed Aylward's submarine was an enemy ship, and for miles they played hide-and-seek with each other. Not until long afterwards, at Fremantle, Aylward discovered that the submarine with which he played almost to Australia was the *Swordfish* which was evacuating Francis B. Sayre, Philippines High Commissioner. The *Swordfish* finally passed the *Sea Raven* while the latter was stalking a Japanese tanker, and arrived in Australia first.

On this journey, Aylward's course took him through Macassar Strait instead of Molucca Passage, on the other side of the Celebes. While in Macassar, the *Sea Raven* surfaced. The quartermaster opened the hatch, as he had done hundreds of times before. As the cover went up, he let out a yell that could be heard all over the submarine. Dozens of wriggling, slippery fish were raining down on him. They poured into the ship, flopping and floundering around the deck. The submarine had come up in the middle of a school of small finny fellows, similar to Spanish mackerel.

"We gathered five or six bucketfuls off topside," Aylward said. "I don't know what kind of fish they were, but they had dark meat and were excellent eating. We all had a good dinner—a regular fish fry."

Although the fishing was good for the submarine, the hunting had been very poor. Not since her encounter with the Japanese task force in the South China Sea had she come upon a likely target. So it was with satisfaction that the officer at the periscope watch, after the submarine had passed Macassar City, observed an enemy tanker loom up out of the mist of a rain squall.

The *Sea Raven* began her approach. Just as she was about to attack, the soundman reported that he heard another ship fairly close. It was on the starboard side and moving in. The submarine let go two torpedoes at the tanker, then dove in a hurry, just in the nick of time. Overhead passed the roaring screws of a big enemy cruiser. If the dive had been a moment later, the submarine would have been rammed.

Only the harrowing sound of the cruiser came to the men deep down in the ocean; there was no comforting blast to show that their hastily dispatched torpedoes had struck the tanker's hull. The soundman was having a busy day. Not long afterward, he reported the sound of breakers.

The *Sea Raven* surfaced and the breakers were there, all right. Long, curling, dangerous ones, too close for comfort; so she cleared the area and moved north again. When the time at last arrived for the *Sea Raven* to come in from her second wartime patrol, she was ordered to Fremantle, at the southwest corner of Australia. This involved passing through the Malay Barrier and into the Indian Ocean. The skipper elected to go through the barrier by way of Sapi Strait, a narrow passage with swift and tricky currents.

"I had about decided to go through at night on the surface," Aylward said, "but my second officer urged that we go through in the daytime, submerged. I finally agreed."

At daylight the submarine dove and started at the north end of the passage. Everything went well until about two o'clock in the afternoon, when they reached the narrowest part of the strait, only about two thousand yards across. Here the submarine caught the full force of the raging current. She went through sideways. It was necessary to steer sixty degrees left in order to make her course. Just as it began to look as if everything was under control, they ran into a large freshwater pocket. The difference in buoyancy between fresh and salt water made itself felt instantly aboard the delicately trimmed underwater craft. With the abruptness of a skyscraper elevator, the submarine dropped. Down, down, she plumped. Those aboard her could have obtained the same sensation by going over Niagara Falls in a barrel. Fortunately, the diving officer was right on the job. He worked fast and effectively. After a drop of about a hundred feet, he caught her, started up again.

"Hold her at fifty!" Aylward shouted.

"I couldn't hold her if I wanted to!" the diving officer yelled back.

The submarine shot on up, popped out onto the foaming sea.

"When we reached the surface, the water in the passage was boiling white," Aylward said. "I've never seen anything to equal it."

In spite of her tossing about, her downs and ups, the American craft managed to negotiate the difficult passage and emerge into the Indian Ocean unscathed. After what she had been through in the preceding weeks, her run into Fremantle was a breeze.

With the exception of the eight days spent at Port Darwin for overhaul and refitting, Aylward had been commanding his submarine on wartime patrol steadily since December 10, when she pulled out through the minefields at Manila. And it was now April. For four long months he had been carrying on his shoulders the final responsibility for the safety and success of the big submarine, operating continuously in enemy waters. The Navy decided Lieutenant Commander Aylward was entitled to a rest in the States—and also to the Navy Cross. At the same time, four members of his rugged crew were advanced in rating.

May 1940 shot of SS-196, *the Sea Raven*, during tests.
Image: Bureau of Ships Collection, U.S. National Archives.

6 – Rescue at Timor

THE *SEA RAVEN*, BY THIS TIME a seasoned veteran of the Pacific war, was overhauled and refitted at Fremantle. Lieutenant Commander Hiram Cassedy took over as her captain. Cassedy, eleven years out of the Naval Academy, was a daring and capable submarine man. It didn't take him long to demonstrate that he was a worthy successor to Aylward.

The *Sea Raven*'s first mission was the same as Lieutenant Commander Fenno had been assigned at Pearl Harbor a couple of months earlier—hauling ammunition to Corregidor. Fenno's submarine *Trout* had delivered artillery shells; the Cassedy submarine was loaded with three-inch antiaircraft ammunition. With nearly the same crew that had prowled the Pacific in her from north of Formosa to Australia, the submarine pulled out of Freemantle and headed north through the Indian Ocean.

Scarcely had her conning tower dipped beyond the horizon when the Navy received a feeble radio message from the Dutch and Portuguese island of Timor, lying some four hundred miles northwest of Australia across the Timor Sea. It was a desperate plea for help from a band of Australians stranded on the beach about twelve miles from Kupang, principal city of the southern Dutch half of the big island. Somehow, these refugees had got hold of a short-wave radio transmitter and were sending frantic code messages, asking that an American warship be sent to rescue them.

This would be a ticklish task. The Japanese had captured Kupang and were swarming over Timor. The skies were full of their planes. Their warcraft were weaving over the waters around the island. And there was a suspicion that the enemy had broken the Australians' code and might be a party to any arrangements for making contact with the castaways. It looked like a better than even chance that a Nipponese reception committee would be awaiting any rescue ship.

Our Navy, however, did not hesitate; it immediately decided to try to get to the Aussies. Cassedy's submarine, loaded with ammunition for Corregidor was the nearest suitable American craft, and by now it was evident that the fall of The Rock at Manila was imminent. Probably the *Sea Raven* could not get the shells there before the Japanese stormed in, so orders buzzed through the air to Cassedy to make the rescue attempt at Timor.

In a lot of ways, our submarines seem to have been the Jacks-of-all-trades for the Navy. They hauled garbage; they hauled ammunition; they hauled treasure. They evacuated high Army and Navy officers and nurses, as well as civilians and civilian officials. They scouted enemy waters and brought back invaluable information. They rescued survivors of ship sinkings who were adrift in lifeboats or on rafts. They snatched Japanese prisoners from the sea and pumped them dry of water and information.

And all the while, they were sinking enemy ships, from spitkits to *marus* to warships. (To a Navy man, a "maru" is any Japanese vessel large enough to escape the derisive name of spitkit.)

Cassedy's mission was the first of its kind for our Submarine Service, but it was not the last. During the Solomons operations, one of our submarines was dispatched to a Japanese-held island in the group to rescue twenty-nine men, women and children. Under cover of darkness, the submarine slipped into the shallow, dangerous waters and kept a rendezvous on schedule. She took off the refugees, among them seventeen white women, right under the noses of the Japanese. And not any too soon.

A day later, an enemy force landed at the spot. Had it not been for the American submarine, those refugees would have become prisoners of the Japanese. Everyone knows what that would have meant. As it was, they were transferred to an American patrol vessel and brought safe to Australia.

The *Sea Raven* also reached the designated point of contact right on time. Moving in at night on the surface, she flashed a recognition signal. From the shore came what appeared to be an answering flash. An eighteen-foot wherry with an engine was put overboard. Almost everyone responded to a call for volunteers. Ensign George Cook, a Reserve officer who was an exceptionally strong swimmer, was selected to lead the party. With him went Joseph McGrievy, a signalman first class, and Leonard Markeson, quartermaster first class.

Bad luck hit them immediately. The engine, in spite of their expert efforts, wouldn't even wheeze. With desperate haste the submariners fashioned paddles and oars from the tops of ammunition boxes. Chief Machinist's Mate T. C. Hall hurriedly made an anchor out of odds and ends of pipe and an old piston. All this consumed precious minutes, but finally the three men in the wherry headed toward the beach.

The surf was high and dangerous, and it was evident that the boat, burdened with the useless engine and propelled by the makeshift sweeps would be unable to negotiate it successfully. Just before they reached the curling white water, Cook called a halt, and the men began to scan the beach from the distance. It was a tight spot. Not only were the Japanese all around, by land, sea and air, but there was a strong current as well as the surf to contend with, and in the water about them they could see sharks which Cook later said were "as big as torpedoes."

Worst of all, no further signals had come from shore. Cassedy, aboard the submarine, was watching the rescue effort with increasing concern. The situation was discouraging and the hour was growing late. Finally he recalled the men in the wherry and the boat was hoisted on deck.

The submarine stood out to sea to charge her batteries while there still was a protecting curtain of darkness. During the day the submarine moved underwater along the shore on an intensive hunt for a sign of the Australians. Through the periscope, Cassedy and his officers scrutinized the beach from Kupang to the point of land which marked their rendezvous spot, but they found nothing to encourage them. Meanwhile some of the crew had been improving the makeshift oars and paddles, and Hall had fashioned some crude oarlocks.

That night the *Sea Raven* surfaced and slipped back to the indicated meeting place. As she drew near, those topside saw a fire burning on the beach, and through the glasses they could make out figures gathered around it. This was what they were looking for, the Americans decided. They broke out the wherry, from which the engine had been removed, and put it overboard. It bobbed alongside, while recognition signals were flashed toward the shore. There was no answering signal, and while the submariners were still trying to establish contact with the group on the beach, a ship was sighted standing out of Kupang and heading toward them close to shore.

The submarine was in a very bad spot. The wherry was over and the deck was covered with men and gear. She was in no condition to make a hurried dive. But fortunately she was lying in a small indentation, almost a bay, in the coast. Everything was secured as rapidly as possible, and the submarine turned a shooting end toward the oncoming vessel, just in case the other ship discovered her and headed in for a fight.

There was a long, pulse-pounding wait as the Japanese craft loomed ever closer. Although those watching her couldn't be certain in the dim light, she appeared to be a destroyer. And then, while the Yanks held their breath, the enemy passed by to seaward without spotting them and faded into the darkness down the coast.

Quickly the men in the submarine rigged up again, and Cook, with the same two petty officers, climbed into the engineless wherry and paddled toward the surf. This time they dropped anchor outside the surf. Although they could see the fire and distinguish the figures easily, repeated signals still brought no reply.

There was a hurried conference in the wherry. Cook announced that he was going to swim in and, disregarding the sharks, he slipped into the water. Battling the surf and the current, he finally managed to crawl up onto the beach, although he had been swept some distance from the point on which the fire had been seen. A flashlight in one hand, a pistol in the other, he started toward it. He had gone only a short distance when he came to a small creek. He waded in and immediately sank to his knees in the muddy bottom; halfway across he tripped and fell sprawling.

When he scrambled up the opposite bank, the ensign was covered with muck and slime from head to foot. As he approached the point, Cook turned the flashlight, which was dimmed with a thin rubber covering, on his face so those about the fire would recognize him as a white man. Confident that the men were the Aussies he sought, he pushed toward them with loud shouts. He got no answer.

Then he suddenly stopped short—for as soon as the group around the fire caught sight of him, they leaped to their feet and ran into the bush. Something was definitely wrong. Completely puzzled and more than a little alarmed, Cook took the only course left to him—he plunged into the sea and fought his way back through the surf and the sharks to the wherry.

Empty handed in spite of all their efforts, the rescue party returned to the submarine. They were received with a sigh of relief by the captain: from the submarine, moving lights had been seen from time to time back in the hills.

Signals had been flashed back and forth, and the Americans suspected that they came from Japanese searching parties, perhaps from enemy tanks beating through the bush. Two attempts to locate the Aussies having been unsuccessful, Cassedy decided to report and get further instructions. He pulled clear of the area and moved down toward Australia in order to be able to transmit his message without disclosing his position to the enemy. The information came back that the Australians had been driven deep into the hills by Japanese searching parties. He was told to return to the rendezvous and try once more to make contact. Two days were consumed in communicating with the base, and when the persistent *Sea Raven* glided in toward the beach of Timor the next time, she got a different reception. Her signals were promptly answered. Yet as the wherry was put over again, the men couldn't help wondering whether the flashes had come from the Aussies or from Japanese who had intercepted the messages and managed to decode them.

Undeterred by these doubts, Cook, McGrievy and Markeson paddled toward the surf. Just outside it, they dropped their makeshift anchor. On the beach they could make out a number of shadowy forms. They called to them, and although neither group could make the other understand what was said through the booming of the surf, the Americans heard enough to realize that at last they had found the castaways.

As before, Cook slipped over the side of the wherry and swam through the surf. He waded out of the water into the midst of thirty-three Australians, most of them members of the Air Force, the others Navy men. Starting with a handful, the party gradually had grown to its present size as more men fleeing the Japanese had joined it. Some of the Aussies had been hiding in the bush as long as eighty-nine days, living on what little food they could get: from friendly natives. They were in pitiful condition. Their clothing was in tatters, and all were suffering from extreme hunger. Some had hideous jungle sores on their legs and arms and only one of them was free from malaria. Three were stretcher cases.

In command of the refugee party was an Australian captain named Rofe. After Cook had explained to him that it would be impossible to bring the wherry through the surf and get it out again, the leader of the Aussies decided to divide his party in half. Cook had brought a line in from his boat, and Rofe directed the sixteen men who were in the best condition to start out, pulling themselves along as well as they could.

They were a plucky lot, those Aussies. So weak they had difficulty even in standing up, they splashed into the sea and one after another faced the boiling surf and the sharks beyond. Cook moved along the line, helping those who showed signs of faltering. As the first of the men approached the wherry, McGrievy and Markeson slid into the water and helped them. Each one had to be boosted into the boat. It was slow and painful work, but at last all sixteen were in the wherry, including the second in command, whom Rofe had sent along while he remained behind. The Americans climbed in after them.

Then they discovered that their makeshift anchor was fouled and couldn't be raised. Cook buoyed it with a life-jacket, and they headed for the submarine. Cassedy, meanwhile, had worked his ship in until it was just skirting the surf, and the rescue party had only a short haul to reach it.

With the Aussies aboard and the wherry securely stowed, the submarine stood out to sea. But before she pulled away, a message was flashed to the little band of men who had been left on the beach. Lieutenant Frank Walker, who had been Aylward's second officer and continued on with Cassedy, told about it.

"We'll be back tomorrow night," the submarine signaled.

From the lonely beach came the answering message in cheerful American slang: "Okay, Yank!"

"They were a game bunch," Walker said. "We knew we'd be back, but those poor fellows on the beach couldn't be sure. But there wasn't a single squawk from any of them."

The next day, Cassedy and Cook went over the situation again and again. Cook pointed out that because of the condition of at least three of the men, one of whom was delirious, it would be necessary to take the small boat through the surf next time. He admitted that getting the wherry to the beach might be more than they could accomplish, not to mention getting it back through the surf loaded down with the helpless men.

It was a difficult decision, but Cassedy made it. For the safety of the majority, he told Cook that he was not to attempt to land the boat. He was to take off as many men as he could get out to it; the others would have to be left to their fate.

When the *Sea Raven* returned to the rendezvous under cover of darkness, her signals were promptly answered by the group on shore, who had spent the day hiding in the bush. A fourth man was added to the wherry's crew this time: John Lorenz, a chief motor machinist's mate. And Hall had fashioned two more anchors, in case they were unable to find the one buoyed to the lifejacket. As it turned out, they couldn't.

At the edge of the surf, the rescuers put out the two new anchors. Lorenz remained in the boat; Cook, accompanied by McGrievy and Markeson, swam ashore. These three men had determined to carry the helpless Aussies out to the wherry on their backs. Cook led off with one of the worst cases. It was a heartbreaking struggle. The dead weight of the sick man forced him under the water almost as much of the time as he was able to keep on the surface.

The surf pounded them back again and again, and beyond the white combers the menacing dorsal fins of the man-eaters sliced through the sea.

Cook finally made it. With Lorenz tugging from within the boat and the ensign pushing from the water, the limp form of the Aussie was hoisted aboard and stretched on the bottom of the wherry.

At that moment, a series of heavy swells rolled in from the sea and smacked the bobbing boat. The two anchors let go. Before either of the Americans could do anything, the wherry had dragged its anchors and was washing into the giant combers. Pitching and rolling, the boat swept through the surf; waves poured over the gunwales and half swamped it. Lying in the bottom, the Australian was choked with the water and almost drowned. Somehow Lorenz and Cook managed to keep the wherry from capsizing, and it finally shot onto the beach.

The action of the sea had nullified Cassedy's orders against landing the boat, and it now looked as if the rescue party was in an even more precarious fix than before. The boat was bailed out and everything made ready for the almost hopeless effort to get through the surf to the waiting submarine. The weakest men were put in the bottom; the others ranged themselves in the water alongside, grasping the gunwales. Rowing, paddling and kicking, the grim-faced men shoved off.

They reached the surf and almost instantly were sent tumbling back. Repeatedly, they drove into the swirling water and repeatedly it pounded them, coughing and choking, back toward shore. Cook declared later that when they started their final effort to break through he had almost decided it was useless. The men at the paddles and oars were exhausted; those in the water could barely hold their grip on the bouncing wherry. And then the sea, just as it had torn the boat from its mooring and pitched it into the surf, by another freakish antic sent them swirling through the white water into the relative calm beyond. A stray eddy or backwash had picked up the wherry and its gasping occupants and flung it through the surf.

A few minutes later, the Aussies were being hauled aboard the big American submarine. The voyage to Australia, which followed, was a nightmare voyage. The officers and crew of the *Sea Raven* gave up their bunks to the starved and fever-racked refugees and slept wherever they could find a corner or a bit of steel deck to stretch out on. When not on watch, they nursed the sick Aussies, dressed their abscesses, under the direction of Chief Pharmacist's Mate Charles Alwin, the submarine's Doc. The only Australian who had escaped malaria on Timor came down with it as they were heading for home.

Several of the rescued men appeared to be hovering between life and death. One in particular was expected to die momentarily, but Alwin gave him close attention and pulled him through. Later, at Perth, the doctors expressed amazement that he had lived. But not a man was lost and all eventually recovered completely.

"Those men were determined not to die after waiting so long to be rescued," Walker said. "They pulled through on their nerve."

The Japanese, according to the Australians, obviously had heard their radio transmitter, because enemy patrols were all around, beating the bush in an effort to locate them. On the other hand, the enemy apparently could not decipher the Aussie code, since they didn't know where the contact was to be made. Friendly natives had brought word to the Aussies that a strange ship was lying off the beach, but by that time Cassedy was heading out to report to his base. The natives had also brought word from the Japanese, advising the Aussies to surrender. The enemy declared their presence was known and even told them how many were in the party.

Excellent treatment had been promised the Australians if they gave up, but they were too familiar with the Japanese to yield to such blandishments. The rescued men had some of the thousands of leaflets dropped by the invaders on the island, leaflets urging the native populace, which is of Malayan, Papuan and Polynesian origin, to come over to them. These propaganda handbills declared that resistance was useless and promised good treatment. They modestly pictured Japan as a nation of humanitarians and philanthropists. But most of the natives refused to be fooled. The Australians were unable to answer the riddle of the men whom Cook scared away from the campfire. The only possible conclusion seemed to be that they were natives who were terrified at the sudden appearance of a strange mud-covered figure in their midst.

It had been a harrowing experience, but it wasn't over yet. The worst stroke of luck was still to come. As the *Sea Raven* was approaching Fremantle, fire broke out in the maneuvering room.

The submarine was badly overloaded with human cargo. Besides that she was carrying tons of shells originally destined for Corregidor—and most of the shells were stored in a compartment next to the one in which the flames burst forth. Nor was it a small fire, but a big and menacing blaze. Without sounding the fire-collision siren for fear of alarming the sick Australians, word was passed to the crew and they began a grim and desperate battle against their newest enemy.

All the power in the submarine was pulled, and for two hours Cassedy and his men fought the licking flames. They got the fire out at last, but when the grimy and exhausted crew relaxed their efforts, their ship was so badly crippled that it could barely crawl through the sea. A call for help was sent by radio to Fremantle.

"We had rescued the Australians from Timor," Walker said, "but now the shoe was on the other foot. The Australians rescued us. They sent out a corvette which reached us the next morning and maneuvered alongside. We were towed majestically into Fremantle." The mission just completed by the *Sea Raven* had called for as much perseverance and initiative, as many difficult decisions, as any adventure in the Pacific in the war. For their part in it, Cassedy and Cook were awarded Navy Crosses; the two men who had accompanied Cook in the wherry,

McGrievy and Markeson, were advanced to chief's rating, and Lorenz received a letter of commendation.

Phillip Morris ad from 1943

7 – Nazi Raider

THE FIRE WHICH BROKE OUT on the *Sea Raven* while the submarine was bringing the rescued Australians home from Timor caused extensive damage. Cassedy's ship was a long time in port, undergoing repairs. By August, however, she was again in fighting trim; her crew were well rested and eager to put to sea. Cassedy shoved off on his second patrol as the *Sea Raven*'s captain and once more he headed for Timor.

The hunting was poor. Although the Americans patrolled the area off the big island for a considerable length of time, they failed to sight any enemy ships. Then one day, just at sunset, the periscope watch spotted a lone merchantman against the blood-red sun. The ship was too far away for the *Sea Raven* to reach while submerged, so she surfaced and gave chase. It was still too light for a direct surface attack, and as the distance between the two craft closed, Cassedy started around her in order to use the concealing shadow of the island in his approach.

The target was a fair-sized vessel. She looked like a setup; almost too easy, Walker declared. While the submarine was lining up her intended prey in the gathering darkness, those aboard the *Sea Raven* heard the sound of depth charges in the distance. They stopped to listen. At the same time, the merchantman came to a dead stop on the calm, oily surface of the sea. Suddenly, the lookout called down that he thought he saw a bow wave. The next instant the bridge of the submarine was flooded with light as a Japanese warship turned a searchlight full upon her.

The submarine made a quick dive. For several hours she was kept down while the Japanese gave her a thorough ash-canning, but she came through undamaged. Nothing daunted, Cassedy kept the *Sea Raven* in the area and watched and waited for the cargo ship, which had been standing into port, to come out. But that was the last they ever saw of their target. And that was the only one they encountered on the patrol. Even Cat Eyes Anastasia—or Kelly—couldn't pick up anything more.

Cat Eyes had been a sergeant in the Coast Artillery and he never let anybody forget it. Nothing on the submarine ever was done exactly to suit him—the way they did it in the CA, as he affectionately called his old outfit. But he turned aside all suggestions that he leave the submarines and go back to the big guns. When some of the boys brought back Army shoes from Corregidor, Cat Eyes bought a pair of them. After that he seemed more satisfied with his lot. The shoes which he wore all the time suited his feet better, he insisted. Made him feel more at home.

On his third patrol in command of the *Sea Raven*, Cassedy was ordered to Sunda Strait, which separates the islands of Sumatra and Java. When the Americans reached the area they discovered a lot of traffic, but they seemed to be on the wrong schedule and were unable to get in range. One long shot was tried but missed the target. Then came the day when the *Sea Raven* was sitting in the center of the strait looking around for Japanese. On the horizon ahead a smudge appeared. Gradually it shaped up as a vessel heading directly toward the waiting submarine. Right down the middle alley, as Walker described it. So far, the *Sea Raven* had sunk no enemy craft under Cassedy's command, although she had carried out one of the most heroic rescues of the war. The tension, perhaps, was a little greater than ordinary as the unsuspecting enemy ship moved nearer, because the chances seemed good that luck was about to change for the better.

Cassedy slipped his submerged fighter across the bow of the oncoming vessel and took up a favorable position. A few minutes later word spread through the crew that they had something out of the ordinary. The suppressed excitement of the submariners at their battle stations was stepped up another notch. Cassedy had obtained a good view of the large flag on the target that was fluttering in the warm tropic breeze. It bore the swastika of the Third German Reich. A strange pigeon had strayed into the Japanese cote.

The order was passed to make ready four tubes. At the eyepiece of the battle periscope stood the submarine's captain, intent and watchful. In front of him at the firing panel was Frank Walker. From the forward torpedo room, the torpedo officer announced that the tubes were ready. Cassedy lined up the target carefully. She was about seven thousand tons, an armed merchant ship, obviously a raider and blockade runner. The skipper's crisp voice broke the silence.

"Stand by one!"

At the fire control panel, Walker connected the firing circuit to tube No. 1 and cut out the others. "One's ready!" Walker said.

"Fire one!"

A tremor ran the length of the *Sea Raven* as the torpedo streaked from its tube.

"One's gone! Two's ready!"

"Fire two!"

"Two's gone! Three's ready!"

"Fire three!"

"Three's gone! Four's ready!"

"Fire four!"

"Four's gone!"

Walker glanced over his shoulder at Cassedy, peering into the periscope.

"Torpedoes away, sir!"

"Secure the tubes!"

The spread of four torpedoes, loaded with hundreds of pounds of destruction, was fanning out toward the Nazi as the American submariners counted the seconds. A muffled explosion came to them. One of the missiles had caught the German ship squarely amidships. It soon became evident to Cassedy at the periscope that the blast had broken her back.

The enemy slowed to a crawl. Although the German appeared to be mortally wounded, the prize was too big to take chances. Two more tubes were made ready; two more torpedoes churned through Sunda Strait toward Hitler's sea rover. Both hit her and she began breaking up. Through their periscope, the submariners could see the Nazi crew lowering lifeboats as their ship settled deeper and deeper.

The Americans watched for a while, then dove. When they came up fifteen minutes later, the German was gone. The *Sea Raven* patrolled for several days without seeing anything she could reach, then headed for home. On the way she passed Christmas Island and paused to scout the vicinity of that British possession held by the Japanese. Christmas is a popular island name with our English cousins. They have one in Nova Scotia, a second in mid-Pacific, south of the Hawaiians, and the third one, which attracted Cassedy's attention, lying in the Indian Ocean, due south of Sunda Strait.

"At first we didn't find anything of interest," Walker said. "We were on the surface at night and all ready to give it up when we suddenly saw lights. They turned out to be from a ship headed into port, which apparently had lit up for recognition. We went back in a hurry."

The *Sea Raven* spent that night loafing outside the harbor at Christmas Island, wondering whether the ship would come out again or stay inside. She stayed inside. At dawn the submarine dove and moved toward the harbor entrance. Cassedy had decided that if the enemy wouldn't come out he was going in. The possibility that the harbor was heavily mined didn't faze him.

Cautiously the submarine maneuvered through the entrance and well inside without detection. Cassedy took his time, made sure of everything before attacking. He brought the ship's stern tubes to bear on the target, with the bow pointed out, ready for a quick getaway. And the target was a good one. Besides, she was squatting in the dock, as motionless as an Egyptian pyramid.

The Japanese had some unusual types of ships, combination craft which they apparently believed were suitable for servicing what they foolishly imagined should be their "sphere of influence." The one Cassedy had caught in its hole was a 10,000-ton combination tanker and transport. She was fast to a pier, on which was a towering railway crane, all set to handle her cargo. The *Sea Raven* let go two torpedoes and ran for the open sea. "The first torpedo broke the ship in half—blew it all to pieces," Walker said. "The second torpedo hit the pier and made matchwood of it. The big railway crane toppled into the water.

"As soon as the Japs could gather their wits, they opened up with shore batteries and threw a lot of shells in our general direction. But we were having breakfast on our way home."

Aboard a submarine on patrol, time gets all tangled up. Nights and days, with their monotonous routine, are just the same to the crew, most of whom never see the sky for weeks on end. Sometimes they aren't even sure whether the ship is diving or surfaced. The natural man to ask about that is a quartermaster. But the *Sea*

Raven's four quartermasters became fed up with their pals approaching them while they were on watch and asking time and again, "Are we divin'?"

On shore leave one day they found the answer to their problem in a Fremantle shop. They bought four caps of the style English schoolboys often wear, with visors both front and back—fore and aft. On one visor the quartermasters printed "submerged" and on the other "surfaced."

Whichever word was on the visor in front, while the wearer was standing watch, indicated the position of the submarine. That ended the questions, and again the resourcefulness of submariners had come to the rescue. With the quartermaster's visor proclaiming that the ship was on the surface, the refitted *Sea Raven* pulled out of Fremantle. She pointed her raking bow toward the area of her fourth, and most successful, patrol under Cassedy's command—off the Palau Islands. Held by the Japanese, the Palaus were an important and heavily defended sea and air base, lying between the Philippine island of Mindanao and the enemy-occupied Carolines.

On the way, the *Sea Raven* looked in at Christmas Island. Cassedy was sick and Walker was in charge of the ship. He sighted nothing in the harbor, but outside discovered a good-sized Japanese cargo ship aground on a reef.

She looked as though she might easily be floated and salvaged, so Walker brought the submarine in close to the beach for a straight shot at the "sitting duck." The torpedo smashed the vessel amidships in the machinery space, and as the submarine cleared the area, the enemy craft was settling deeper and listing badly. What was left of her wasn't worth a salvage effort.

Pushing on toward their station, the Americans passed close to the island of Amboina and there they picked up what appeared to be the smoke of a convoy on the horizon.

But after studying the promising prospect, Cassedy, now recovered from his illness, decided that the convoy for some reason had stopped. He tried to close on it, but without result. Just when it began to look as if things were hopeless, the Japanese ships started to come over the horizon, bearing directly toward the *Sea Raven*. This was tops in good luck—the convoy consisted of five freighters, escorted by two patrol boats, or corvettes, and a light destroyer.

Captain Cassedy sneaked his submerged ship across the course of the oncoming enemy vessels, passing very close to one of the corvettes. Once inside the screen of the convoy, he fired three torpedoes.

Two of the tin fish struck home in the destroyer; the third blew up with a terrific explosion in the hull of one of the freighters. No sooner had the torpedoes cleared the submarine than the skipper's order rang through the battle phones: "Secure the tubes! Take her down and rig for depth charge!"

The Americans knew what was coming—and they got it. The two corvettes buzzed angrily back and forth, dumping ashcans all around. But the *Sea Raven* slipped out from under and continued on her course toward her area of patrol.

The trip was uneventful until she reached the vicinity of Palau. Then, just at dusk, she sighted a pair of ships heading out. By the time the submarine had made her approach it was pitch dark. She fired one torpedo and missed. As soon as she worked clear, she surfaced and took after the two Nipponese freighters.

By the light of dawn she picked up the quarry again. Meanwhile the Japanese had acquired an escort of a couple of patrol vessels. Cassedy nevertheless managed to slip in and cut loose with two torpedoes at each of the cargo ships. Then he took the *Sea Raven* deep. As the submarine dodged the depth-charging, the cheering sound of two explosions could be heard plainly. Which of the torpedoes hit what, the Americans never learned. When they finally surfaced, neither the freighters nor their escort was in evidence. The only craft in sight was a freighter coming from the opposite direction, but she was out of range. The submarine patrolled the vicinity hopefully all the rest of the day. But she found no more targets for her tubes and with the coming of night headed back toward Palau.

That night she picked up another convoy and trailed it through the darkness. By daylight, there it was, made to order for the submarine—five cargo ships, guarded by three corvettes.

Cassedy closed in on the cluster of targets, but this time he elected to fire from outside the screen of escorts. Three torpedoes were sent streaking toward the largest merchant ship and one toward a corvette. Three of the four found their marks. The freighter caught two and the patrol ship stopped the other.

"Our little friends were pretty active," Walker said, "and we had to get out of the way of their ash-canning. But on our sound gear we could hear the merchant ship breaking up. After a while we came up for a peek through the periscope. There were only two corvettes, and they were busy picking up survivors from the cargo ship. The third was nowhere in sight, so it's probable that we got him."

The *Sea Raven* moved back in closer to Palau and continued her patrol. For a couple of days nothing happened. Then about one o'clock in the morning she picked up a ship—big and pretty. Although there was a moon, it was hazy as the submarine closed the target. Not until she was lining the lone vessel up did she see the big red cross on her side. "We took her picture and went on our way," Walker said.

The submarine's supply of torpedoes was running low, and Captain Cassedy was beginning to think about starting for home. The hunting had been good; enemy game on two occasions had been encountered in coveys, and the undersea hunters had blasted away at them with marked success. And then what should appear on the horizon but a third convoy! It was composed of four or five large freighters and two destroyers.

The *Sea Raven*'s forward tubes were empty but three torpedoes were left in the stern. While the convoy was still some distance away, the submarine crossed ahead of it in order to bring the after tubes to bear. The Americans knew that this would be their final attack on this patrol. They were anxious to make it a bang-up one. Cassedy waited until the destroyer on the starboard was only five hundred yards away. Then he fired two torpedoes at the biggest ship, which was the second in line. The submariners heard them both hit, but after that everyone was occupied with other matters.

"Those Jap merchant ships must have had valuable cargoes," Walker said, "because they had their first team escorting them, including planes. They dropped their first bomb almost down the hatch. Luckily it didn't do any damage. But those destroyers gave us a hot time. We could tell they were on the first team by the way they played."

After a long time, the Japanese faded away. Cassedy lifted the *Sea Raven*'s defiant and dripping bow to the surface of the Pacific and pointed it on the long-haul home to Pearl Harbor. The sturdy American submarine had wound up fourteen months of almost constant hunting in Japanese waters—from the moment the war began. She had a bagful of Japanese ships to her credit. And the *Sea Raven* herself was unscratched by the enemy. It took an atom bomb in the tests at Bikini Atoll after the war to end her career.

Construction of observation towers in preparation for the Bikini Atoll tests

8 – Our Submarines Were Ready

THE OUTBREAK OF HOSTILITIES WITH Japan found the submarines attached to our Pacific Fleet ready. In the light of the job they were called on to do, there weren't many of them, but their officers and men had been operating under war routine for months. They were at peak efficiency and thoroughly conditioned to the hardships and strain of undersea operations during wartime. Other arms of the services, land and sea, took a terrific beating when the Japanese sneaked in on Pearl Harbor, but the enemy didn't find our submarines lined up like a row of pigeons, waiting to be knocked off. Our submarines were ready and eager; they were out pitching torpedoes into Japanese hulls while other branches of our Army and Navy were still attempting to catch their breath.

Not one American submarine was damaged when the enemy rained destruction from the skies on our great Pacific naval base in Hawaii. At Manila Bay, the story was the same, except that after the war was well under way we did lose a submarine at the Cavite navy yard. But it was not because she was caught off guard. She was damaged by bombs, and was destroyed by our own forces to keep her from falling into the hands of the enemy when the defense of the Philippines collapsed. Also, this particular submarine was in drydock at the time of the bombing, and no one has yet figured out evasion tactics for a ship out of water.

There was nothing mysterious or accidental about the magnificent performance of our Pacific submarines. The Japanese did not surprise our undersea fleet, because it was, for the most part, out on patrol. Its ships were scattered off Midway and Wake and Guam, through the Philippines and in the South China Sea— deployed in strategic areas which the warlords of Nippon had been claiming as solely the property of the Son of Heaven. The number of submarines tied up on that fateful Sunday morning in Hawaii could easily have been counted on one hand. There was some good fortune about the smallness of their number, but the Japanese would never have found many more at the dock. It simply was not the practice of our Submarine Command at Pearl Harbor to keep a submarine in port if the ship and its crew were in condition to be out on patrol. Most of our Pacific Fleet submarines learned that we were at war through official radio messages received in lonesome wastes of the ocean, not by seeing the rising sun on airplanes overhead or hearing the crash of bombs around them.

So our submarines were ready in the Pacific. And because they were ready and forewarned, their achievements were the most amazing and effective of any naval force in history. Even though the strength of the Submarine Service was small in proportion to that of the surface and air arms, three out of every four of Japan's vital merchant ships that were sunk were sent to the bottom by American submarines! Almost one out of every two enemy combat vessels sunk received its death blow from one of our submarines. And only about one and one-half percent of the total Navy personnel in 1945 was in the Submarine Service.

There weren't many—but the few were mighty. The Pacific Ocean, the main arena for the war against the Japanese, is the largest of all the world's great water areas. It covers about 68,634,000 square miles, which is a formidable body of ocean merely as a question of transit. Even by air its crossing is a lengthy business; on the surface the voyage normally lasts for weeks. To traverse it partly underwater, as our submarines had to, required time and patience in large quantities.

To cope with all this ocean, from the standpoint of submarine operations, at the start of the war the United States had an undersea fleet of one hundred and thirteen ships in commission, seventy-three listed as building, and Congress had appropriated funds for one hundred to one hundred fifty more. Exactly how many submarines Japan had then has not been disclosed, but it is understood that her submarine force was numerically at least equal to our own, not counting the midget submarines she had. These, however, turned out to be of little importance.

American submarine strength was impressive on paper, but the majority of our ships were of the vintage of World War I; they were relatively small, out of date, and limited in range and offensive power. We had some of the big, modern fleet submarines in service, to be sure, but it was not until the early part of 1943 that we began launching them in sizable numbers. As far back as the beginning of 1941, the Submarine Service at Pearl Harbor rolled up its sleeves and went into intensive training for a fight.

The higher officers of the Submarine Command never doubted that war with Japan would come sooner or later—probably much sooner than the American people and many responsible officials in Washington expected. These officers had been in the Orient for long stretches, most of them, and they had seen much and heard more. On the China Station, on their occasional visits to Japan itself with units of our fleet, they had come in contact with the Nipponese; they had observed and studied them at close range and as a result they mistrusted them.

For years, whenever officers of our Pacific warships had gathered in their wardrooms for a session of scuttlebutt, the conversational needle had inevitably swung to the magnetic north of one topic—war with Japan. If this was true of the surface craft, it was doubly true of the submarines.

The men in the submarines realized that when war came our undersea fleet would for the first time in history have a chance to prove its mettle and full worth.

When the submarines attached to the Pacific Fleet began their extensive and intensive training many months before Pearl Harbor, the first thing they did was to jettison the leisurely, even though thorough, methods of peacetime.

The Commander of Submarines, Pacific Fleet, at that time and until May 1942, was Rear Admiral Thomas Withers, whose firsthand experience in submarines covered almost thirty years, beginning with the E-boats, which were laid down in 1908. There was probably no man living at that time with a wider practical background in the operation of undersea craft or a better grasp of their problems and strategy. Among other things, Admiral Withers instituted a program of testing and toughening ships and personnel. One of its main points was that our submarines should always operate, while on patrol, under war conditions.

Previously, during peacetime, a dive of several hours had been considered long enough for training and practice. The cruises—or patrols, as they are called— lasted two or three weeks, seldom longer. When our submarines went under they usually submerged to periscope depth and called it a dive. Periscope depth is the depth at which the extended periscope sticks a couple of feet above the surface.

In our older ships it was about forty feet, in our new ones, about sixty-five. Only rarely did our submariners dive as deep as one hundred feet and not once in three years would they submerge to two hundred feet. Such a dive was something to write home about in those days.

Under the new system, however, the COMSUBPAC—the Navy way of condensing Commander of Submarines, Pacific Fleet—ordered the length of the patrols by our submarines stepped up. The ships were directed to follow the routine of wartime in enemy waters, submerging by day and running on the surface at night and recharging their batteries. All dives were to be quick ones, the kind a submarine must make when an enemy destroyer is bearing down on it at thirty-five or forty knots or an enemy plane is roaring out of the sky. The captains were ordered to go to one hundred feet on every dive and at least once on each patrol to submerge to two hundred feet.

Our submarines were sent out from Pearl Harbor for six weeks at a time, and then for two months or even longer. At the start and finish of the patrols, the mental and physical condition of the personnel was carefully checked. The approximate point at which the men began to go stale and the length of patrol which gave the maximum effectiveness were established. None of the test patrols were pushed to the actual point where the crew cracked up, but the time it would take before the human factor gave way was pretty well indicated.

The question of the best diet for submarine personnel was given careful study. Vitamin experiments were undertaken, including the use of vitamin A, the so-called night blindness vitamin, as an aid to the lookouts on night watches. The problem of recreation and relaxation within the extremely limited space of a submarine received attention and record-playing machines, reading matter, games— everything possible to alleviate the hardships of undersea life—were provided. Later, after war began, the Royal Hawaiian Hotel in Honolulu was taken over by the Navy, and on their return from patrols the submarine crews went there to rest, recuperate, and enjoy themselves for ten days or two weeks. A relief crew took over the routine port duty aboard the submarine while she was being overhauled and refitted.

Other aspects of submarine operation in wartime also were given careful attention long before the war. Pearl Harbor submarines worked hard and long on communications, with a full appreciation of the vital part this factor would play in wartime. Admiral Withers made frequent talks before the submarine captains, emphasizing that they must prepare their minds for war and prepare the minds of their men likewise. He not only spoke to them in groups but had long talks with the skippers individually.

There were many sessions of "skull practice," as the football squads call it—meetings at which problems were discussed by the submariners and the Admiral, his staff and Captain (later Rear Admiral) Freeland A. Daubin and Captain Allan R. McCann, a squadron commander. The Flag Office at Pearl Harbor became a school of high-pressure training for war.

Everything short of declaring hostilities was done to make the men in our Pacific submarines ready for the day that finally came. Their ships were depth-charged to get them used to that unpleasant experience. The charges were dropped far enough away to be harmless, but close enough to give a good idea of what the real thing was going to be like. Submarine captains were taught, by actual experience, the depths necessary to avoid detection from the sky. They were bombed. Planes were sent aloft with orders to let go on any submarine they could spot beneath the surface. The bombs were real, though too small to cause damage if they hit, and on at least one occasion a submarine surfaced with an unexploded bomb resting on its deck.

It was Spartan training, but it paid big dividends. Our submarines were ready to fight the minute the bell rang. They were ready to bear up under war conditions, because war conditions had been their routine for many months. They were able to make long patrols immediately, because long patrols were their custom. They started sinking enemy ships without delay, and the submarines from Pearl Harbor made the long haul to the coast of Japan and sank Japanese ships in their home waters in the early days of the war, although the press reports erroneously gave credit to the submarines of the Asiatic Fleet, based at Manila.

All this prewar training and toughening was not given to a run-of-the-mill personnel. The Submarine Service is a compact, and to some extent independent, organization. Its officers and men are all volunteers. They've not only had to pass stringent physical examinations but also prove their emotional stability, and with few exceptions they have gone through the Submarine School. The enlisted men are almost all specialists and are constantly undergoing further specialized instruction. If any one arm of the service could lay claim to having the cream of our naval manpower, the Submarine Service's claim would rest on a firm basis.

In World War I, Germany almost beat Britain by means of submarines alone, but the Germans made a major mistake, which possibly cost them the war. It was a mistake the Allies realized, although the enemy himself apparently did not recognize it until too late. The methodical Germans concentrated on the machine and neglected the man.

They constructed U-boats of unsurpassed effectiveness at the time, then tried to operate them with crews that were temperamentally unfit, poorly or only partly trained, and gave those crews conditions aboard that increased instead of eased the unavoidable strain and tension of submarine life in wartime.

Germany's U-boats in World War I stood up, but the men who manned them broke down. Our Submarine Command made no such mistake. Personnel always had been and always will be all-important. As to our submarines themselves, their potential performances within their allotted margins of safety were known. That was something that could be figured out mathematically by the designers, although the ability of the ships to absorb punishment beyond the margin of safety, when forced to, produced some heartwarming surprises. The ability of their crews to bear up under the mental and nervous pressure, the physical grind of week after week at sea, much of the time under the sea, was the main question. And the Pacific Submarine Command found the answer—many months before the war—when it ceased dummy dives, dummy patrols, and dummy maneuvers.

On that peaceful Sunday morning when the Japanese bombers swept in from the sea at Pearl Harbor, our submarine men were fit, eager, and on the job. They had yet to experience the nerve-racking ordeal of a depth-charge attack by the enemy and they had yet to feel the tremendous thrill that comes when your own torpedo explodes in the vitals of an enemy ship, but everything humanly possible had been done to put them in fighting trim. Their submarines had fuel and stores for long patrols and a select and efficient personnel conditioned to long periods at sea. All the Navy had to tell them was to start shooting.

9 - Vendetta

WHEN A MAN VOLUNTEERS FOR DUTY in the Submarine Service but is rejected either for physical reasons or as temperamentally unsuited, there is no stigma attached to his rejection. It signifies only that the applicant does not have the physical, nervous or emotional makeup to withstand the conditions peculiar to living and fighting underwater. He may be an excellent man on a surface warship; just as a man may be a misfit as a pilot of a fast fighter plane, but make an excellent bomber pilot or bombardier.

No one appreciates this better than the top officers of the Submarine Service. Some years ago, when Admiral Withers was a division commander in the Submarine Service, he headed a board of examiners passing on the qualifying of submarine officers. He noticed that one of the officers up for qualifying answered some of the questions rather strangely. Withers took him aside and asked him what was on his mind. The young officer took a deep breath.

"Commodore," he said, "I come from Gloucester, Massachusetts. All my family have gone to sea as far back as I know. But it makes my flesh creep to go down in a submarine."

Withers nodded thoughtfully. "Why did you get into them?"

"I was assigned to them. I'll go anywhere. But it still makes my flesh creep to go down in a submarine."

"Well, I'll see that you're assigned to a surface ship."

The young officer shook his head. "No, I'll go in the submarines. I wouldn't want anything said about me."

"Don't worry," Withers reassured him, "nothing will be said."

The man was sent to a cruiser, according to the Admiral, and was one of the best officers on the ship. He would have been doomed to failure as a submarine officer. There was nothing against him; he was merely temperamentally unsuited for the service, though a first-class man.

Incidentally, the rank of Commodore, corresponding to that of brigadier general in the Army, was abandoned in 1899. It was restored by Act of Congress in April 1943. During the intervening years, however, squadron and division commanders were frequently addressed as "Commodore."

Quite obviously, anyone with a strong dislike for close confinement might develop a dangerous state of mind if compelled to stay within the restricting steel of a submarine's hull for long periods. This type rarely gets by the searching tests given applicants, but it did happen now and then during the war and on occasion resulted in the misplaced unfortunate completely "blowing his top."

Aboard a submarine, where the safety of all may well depend on the stability and efficiency of each, they cannot afford to have any square pegs in round holes.

The entire officer and enlisted personnel must fit snugly into place. Since the Submarine Service is known to be dangerous, arduous, and much of the time tedious, it is interesting to discover the motives which prompted some of our submariners to volunteer in the first place. Certainly the service never made the slightest effort to glamorize itself. It never called on Hollywood, the radio, or the pages of our newspapers and magazines to picture life in the undersea service as a mere strutting around in a snappy uniform. No popular songwriter ever composed a sentimental ballad entitled "He Wears a Pair of Hungry Dolphins."

Guts without glamour have brought the Submarine Service to its peerless standing. Some of our submariners frankly admit they were attracted in the first place by the fifty percent extra pay that goes with undersea duty. To others, the relatively informal type of discipline made an appeal. Submarine discipline is, in many ways, more rigid than on a battleship; but it is strictly functional; discipline with a definite purpose. There is a minimum of drill for drill's sake and officers and men in the cramped quarters of a submarine, in constant peril from the elements as well as the enemy, are brought into a close relationship which increases their mutual understanding and respect.

Paradoxically, a submarine crew is a compact unit, almost a single entity, and yet the members seem to retain a higher degree of rugged individuality than in any other arm of the service. Each man is a cog in the human mechanism that operates the undersea craft, but he is proudly aware that, whatever his rank or rating, he is a vital cog.

Literally, there is no room in a submarine for any other kind. A modern submarine has more intricate machinery, and more of it, than any other class of ship. To look at it one way, a submarine consists of about five million dollars' worth of machinery wrapped up in a fairly small steel hull. Operating and death-dealing machines fill the ship; the men, when at sea, eat and sleep, work and play in the scanty space between the machines. Since love of machinery is an outstanding trait of American boys, more than one who joins the Navy is irresistibly drawn to a submarine by its very construction.

In time of war, however, another motive moves men to serve in the submarines. As the submariners put it, they'd rather dish it out than take it. A submarine is built primarily for attacking.

That was the case with Wilson McSwain, motor machinist's mate second class, who was on a destroyer during the Pearl Harbor raid. On one patrol later on, between Midway and Wake, McSwain declared his ship dodged eighteen torpedoes from Japanese submarines. So right after participating in the raid on the Gilbert and Marshall Islands, he put in for the submarines in order to pitch rather than catch. Then there was William H. Kremin, fireman first class, a member of Mike Fenno's crew. Kremin also was on a destroyer, a sister ship of the ill-fated *Kearny*.

While on Atlantic patrol, October 17, 1941, the *Kearny* was attacked by a U-boat and torpedoed; eleven members of the crew were killed. Kremin says that after he saw what the Nazi torpedoes had done to the *Kearny*, he decided he'd rather be firing the tin fish than stopping them. He applied for a transfer. These reasons for volunteering to serve in the Submarine Service would probably cover most of the men in the service. But they didn't apply to Lieutenant (j.g.) Robert M. McKellar, USNR, a V-7 officer from San Leandro, California. McKellar was probably the only man on record to employ a submarine as a weapon in conducting a vendetta.

The story began in Boston, when the young Reserve officer was assigned to a trawler which had been converted into an antisubmarine patrol boat. After the Navy took over the former fishing craft, the ship's name was dropped, and it received a number as one of our YP (yacht patrol) fleet. She was the *YP-389*. McKellar was the engineering officer. However, since this YP carried only three commissioned officers and twenty-one enlisted men in her crew, mostly Reserves, he doubled as the navigation and gunnery officer. The ship was wide of beam and about one hundred twenty-five feet long. She had a single diesel engine, which enabled her to mog along like a fat old lady, and with only slightly more speed. But she had a lot of good in her. She could take rough weather in her stride, and she was comfortable if not fast.

The YP trawler's job was to locate Nazi submarines when they stuck their periscopes up in our Atlantic coastal waters. Then, if her ashcans didn't get results, she would radiophone for help in the task of disposing of the enemy. McKellar's heavy-weather craft was dispatched to an area where the hunting looked promising. The U-boats were lurking around the shipping lanes off Cape Hatteras, a place notorious for the frequency and fierceness of the storms that sweep over it. And toward Cape Hatteras, the graveyard of many a gallant ship both steam and sail, the YP trawler pursued her stolid course.

All went well with the converted fisherman for quite a while, except for the weather. Then, to the relief of the crew, the weather took a turn for the better. The sea became so calm a man could stay in his bunk without holding on.

"On this particular night," McKellar said, "I was off watch and asleep, when I was awakened by the sound of the general alarm. The clanging of the bell lifted me right out of my bunk and onto my feet. The instant I hit the deck, I scrambled into my shoes and pants.

"My bunk was right beside the ladder which led to the bridge. It didn't take me long to reach topside. The general quarters bell was still ringing as I climbed onto the bridge, where the captain was on watch."

The captain was Lieutenant Roderick Phillips, of New York City.

"It was about two o'clock. The moon had just gone down and it was dark as pitch. But the sea was fairly smooth. One of the first things I heard was the chattering of a machine gun."

Somewhere off there in the darkness, McKellar learned quickly, was a German submarine, but his straining eyes failed to make it out immediately.

"I saw McLean, a seaman first class, at the companionway into the crew's quarters," McKellar said. "McLean was an old Navy man who had gone into the Merchant Marine after his hitch, but had re-enlisted in the Navy and joined our ship just before we headed south from Boston.

"I heard him shout into the crew's quarters. 'This is the real thing!' he called out. Then he started toward his station. At that moment there was a bright flash off the starboard quarter from the Nazi submarine out there in the night. It was a direct hit—right in the companionway where the men were coming out.

"I never saw McLean again," McKellar continued. "That first shell from the enemy either killed or critically wounded several men. He must have been blown overboard.

"The captain passed the word to get the depth charges ready, and I made my way aft. At his station at the depth-bomb racks, I found Wilson Cole, a fireman. I gave him the depth at which to set the charges, then started forward again. Meanwhile, our forward machine guns had opened fire on the submarine. Both machine guns were raking the enemy."

The battle between the patrol trawler and the U-boat became a running fight in the darkness off Cape Hatteras. The one-time fishing boat was putting out all she had, but she didn't have much. She was outgunned by the submarine, which was pouring both shells and machine-gun fire at her. It was a one-sided battle, but the YP refused to give up, even though she was unable to use her major weapon, the depth bombs, with the submarine on the surface. Cole was sticking grimly to his post at the stern, in the hope that sooner or later a chance might come to dump the TNT on the Germans. "Just as I started forward," McKellar said, "the after machine-gunner, Robert Wilson, fell wounded in both arms and the head. Another man jumped into his place and kept the gun firing.

"We were all working frantically, hauling up ammunition, caring for the wounded as best we could. While I was at the stern, standing close to Cole and a fireman named Crabb, a shell burst almost on top of us. Both Cole and Crabb were killed. By some miracle, I escaped with only shrapnel wounds."

For half an hour the uneven battle continued. For an hour. Meanwhile, the trawler had sent in a report on the radiotelephone. A little later she had called again, this time asking for help. But no help was forthcoming.

"The sub had holed us at the waterline," McKellar said. "We were beginning to settle. But we still hung on and were putting up a pretty good fight. Then the Nazis planted one good shot in the engine room that set off the fire-extinguisher system and filled the place with carbon dioxide. From then on, no one could stay there."

The crew came up on deck and waited grimly. After an hour and a quarter, the YP trawler had settled so low that her well deck was awash. It was evident her fighting days were almost over. Captain Phillips passed the word to abandon ship.

With the enemy still pounding away with shells and machine-gun fire, the crew "stepped over the side" in their life jackets.

"We placed Wilson, the wounded gunner, in a life preserver and the first group took him with them," McKellar said. "After we abandoned ship, the submarine approached to within fifty yards and continued to throw shells into the trawler."

When all her crew, except the six who had been killed, had left her, the valiant trawler slipped from sight. "There were half a dozen men in the group I was with in the water," McKellar said. "Every one of us had a wound of some kind. As a matter of fact, besides the men killed, not a person aboard the ship had escaped injury in the battle. We drifted around in the darkness, keeping in touch with each other and hoping to see a rescue ship. About dawn we sighted a Coast Guard patrol boat, which we learned later had been sent out for us. But she didn't see us, and we were unable to attract her attention. It was a bad moment.

"However, after we had been in the water about four hours, we were sighted by planes and picked up. Wilson, the wounded gunner, was rescued with the other group and eventually recovered.

"While we were drifting around in the water, I had plenty of chance to think things over," McKellar said. "I decided I'd just as soon be down below taking a crack at the enemy. Right then, I made up my mind I'd try to get in the submarines, and I finally managed it. They've made a little brass plaque here at the navy yard for me. It's about four by five inches. At the top is inscribed: A SHIP FOR A MAN."

Beneath this caption McKellar had had engraved the names of the six men who lost their lives when the Nazi submarine shelled and sank the YP-389 off Cape Hatteras.

They were:

R. MCLEAN, SEAMAN FIRST CLASS
MAGNUS HIA, SEAMAN SECOND CLASS
CHARLES HENSLEY, SEAMAN SECOND CLASS
WILSON B. COLE, FIREMAN THIRD CLASS
VINCENT W. CRABB, JR., FIREMAN SECOND CLASS
JOHN DOUCETTE, FIREMAN THIRD CLASS

"Each time the submarine I'm now assigned to sinks a ship," McKellar said, "I'll put a star in front of a name, until we've chalked up six enemy ships for those six men. A ship for a man!"

McKellar, when he told his story, was commissary officer and assistant torpedo and gunnery officer on the *Sawfish*, one of our big, deadly fleet submarines.

"My battle station is at the forward torpedo tubes," he said, with obvious satisfaction. "Right where I can see those fish go out!"

In the months that followed, the submarine *Sawfish* ranged the Pacific, hunting and sinking Japanese ships. McKellar had more than enough stars for his vendetta plaque.

10 – Attack and Getaway

ONE DIVISION OF OUR SUBMARINES, attached to the Asiatic Fleet, had been out on torpedo practice the first week in December 1941. At 3:45 a.m. on December 8, while lying in Mariveles, just outside Manila Bay, the men in these ships realized that the warm-up was over.

The game had begun.

When the word came from Pearl Harbor that the Japanese had bombed our base there, the officers and men of the submarine *USS Pickerel* were thankful for one thing: their wives and families had been moved out of the Philippines the year before. Everyone on the submarine worked furiously taking on torpedoes and stores for what lay ahead.

They continued to get reports on the disaster at Hawaii. Mounting anger at the Nipponese treachery fired their determination to get at the enemy as fast as they could find him. Lieutenant Commander Barton E. Bacon, Jr., from Rockwood, Tennessee, was captain of the *Pickerel*. By late afternoon, December 8, Bacon's ship was ready for sea and for war. She cleared the minefields and got out just at dark, heading for the coast of French Indo-China, eight hundred miles to the west. It took her three days to reach the area, and she ran into nothing on the way except rough and disagreeable weather.

For a couple of weeks the Americans patrolled up and down the coast. They found no Japanese ships for their torpedoes and later learned that troopships bound for Malaysia had already gone through. Finally, they encountered a patrol vessel, fired one torpedo, and missed.

Christmas Day was spent submerged. With Japanese ships to be sunk, the crew displayed little interest in the occasion, although they enjoyed a good Christmas dinner. Bert Smith, a seaman first class, did his best to work up a Yuletide spirit by drawing a large picture of a Christmas tree which he hung in the mess-room.

From the Indo-China coast, the *Pickerel* headed back to the Philippines. She patrolled off Caba at the northern end of Lingayen Gulf; then she moved down the coast and back into Mariveles. In the weeks she had been away, things had gone from bad to worse. Japanese planes were bombing steadily. The submarine lay on the bottom all day and worked at night overhauling and refitting. The valiant crew of the submarine tender *Canopus* worked feverishly and courageously, servicing the ships at Mariveles night and day. They knew they were expendable and would have to stay to the bitter end. But although a tender may be expendable, the submarines themselves certainly are not. Their job is to attack and sink enemy ships and then to get away with a whole skin, not stick around and sacrifice themselves.

At this time Bacon added an officer and nine extra men to the complement aboard his submarine. Most of them were from the *Sea Lion*, which the Japanese bombers had hit in drydock at the Cavite Naval Base and which the United States Navy subsequently destroyed. The *Sea Lion*'s personnel was distributed among other submarines. One of the men who joined Bacon's ship was Chief Yeoman W. L. Prickett, a Georgian. He had been in the Navy twenty-two years. During nine of them he had been in submarines, and he had served three tours of duty on the Asiatic Station. Prickett was the chief yeoman in charge of the Flag Office of Captain John Wilkes, Commander of Submarines, Asiatic Fleet, aboard the submarine tender *Holland*. After war started, the Flag Office was moved to the port area of Manila. This was an uncomfortable spot because there was no air-raid protection; when the bombers came over, everyone had to sprint from the area to the shelters in the town. On some days, when the Japanese raided seven or eight times, the men at the Flag Office had to step lively.

"We always used to pick the time right after a raid to take our showers," Prickett said, "but one day the Japs made a quick return. They caught me taking a bath. I lit out for the protection of the town—and all I had on was a pair of skivvies, a helmet, a gas mask and a forty-five strapped around my waist. But you don't worry much about what you're wearing at a time like that.

"Another day, we had a very short warning. I was right out in the open between the port area and the town when the bombs began to fall. It didn't look as if there was a bit of protection anywhere around. Then I saw a freshly dug hole and jumped into it."

Prickett discovered the hole was half full of water. It also contained a steel box, about four or five feet square. While the raid was going on, he crouched beside the box, and before he started to climb out of his impromptu shelter he decided to investigate it. He lifted the lid and looked in.

"I think that was about the biggest scare of the war for me," Prickett said. "The box was full of—detonators! A bomb anywhere near would have set them off. The danger was over by then, but the sight of all those detonators which I'd been leaning against made me so weak I couldn't climb out of the hole. So I blew my whistle."

At the sound of the chief's whistle, a couple of Filipino soldiers came running up.

"What's the matter, cheep?" they asked. The chief explained. They pulled him, dripping wet and breathless, out of the hole.

"You wouldn't believe it, but I crawled a couple of blocks on my hands and knees before I could get my breath back," Prickett said.

On Christmas Eve the Japanese bombers went to work on the port area with highly destructive results. Prickett wasn't in the shower on this occasion; fortunately, too, because he lost all the clothes he wasn't wearing. Manila was about to be declared an open city, and the Navy men at the ruined port area were ordered evacuated. By tug, lighter and submarine tender, Prickett journeyed to Bataan. There he joined in handling supplies and taking them into the hills for MacArthur's men to use later in their bitter stand against the invaders.

On December 29, he stepped aboard Bacon's submarine. Another man who joined Bacon's crew as an extra was Raymond G. Way, a signalman first class. Submarines were old stuff to Way. Of his nine years in the Navy, he had spent six and a half in undersea craft, serving on eight different ships. He had been attached to the *Sea Lion* when she was hit by bombs while in drydock.

"We'd been working all night on the ship," Way said, "and I was sound asleep in the barracks when the Japs came over, about noon. I hit the deck and went back to my sub and stayed there. While the raid on Cavite was going on, I was in the radio room, listening to Don Bell at the Manila radio station describing it. He was twenty miles away and telling what he saw through a window. We were right in the middle of it. Incendiaries and demolition bombs were dropping all around.

"The Japs made two flights over, lasting about thirty minutes. The tug next to us was hit. A little later, I heard a loud slapping noise almost overhead. I knew we'd been hit, too, but I didn't realize how close the bomb had struck until I smelled it.

"We salvaged the motors and confidential gear," Way said. "All the rest was destroyed. A lot of fires had been started, and we were kept busy fighting them."

Way put up at the enlisted men's club until December 24, when the Cavite personnel was evacuated. He, like Prickett, was moved over to Bataan, where he filled sandbags and cached supplies for the Army back in the hills.

"There were a lot of rumors around," Way said. "One of them was that the aircraft carrier *Ranger* was off Corregidor. That made us feel pretty good. We figured it would keep the Japs off. But it was only a daydream. The reports we got that the Japs were closing in, however, were true." When it was decided to evacuate most of the submarine personnel, Way drew the ship commanded by Bacon and went aboard on the 29th.

The following day, Bacon brought his submarine up from the bottom where it was lying for protection, and took a look around through his periscope. Planes were everywhere, enemy planes that were dumping their bomb cargoes persistently on Mariveles. They set the place afire and burned it out. The *Canopus* received a hit, but she went right on servicing the submarines. Mention of that rugged tender is enough to bring cheers from any of the officers and men who were in the Asiatic Fleet's submarines during those disheartening days. *Canopus* is the name of a star of the first magnitude visible in the southern heavens; the tender *Canopus* was a star of the first magnitude in the Submarine Service, shining brightly to the very last.

On the morning of December 31, Bacon took the *Pickerel* out of the ruins of Mariveles and headed down through the middle of the Philippines on patrol. New Year's Day was spent off Bondoc Peninsula. Sighting nothing, he proceeded to Cebu and then to Zamboanga, on the southern tip of the island of Mindanao.

From there he moved across the Celebes Sea and into Molucca Passage. He was headed for Port Darwin, Australia, hunting Japanese on the way, when he received orders to return to Davao in the Philippines, where the enemy was affecting landings.

The crew had made all preparations for the Neptune ceremony as the ship crossed the equator. When the new orders arrived, the *Pickerel*'s nose was almost on the line, so Bacon pushed ahead. The submarine crossed the equator twice within a few minutes, down and back, and the novices aboard were duly initiated.

So far the *Pickerel* had sunk no enemy shipping, but her luck took a quick change for the better. As she was entering Davao Gulf, about two o'clock in the morning, she sighted a *maru*. She made a perfect approach, slipping within range of the target undetected. Two torpedoes boiled through the bay toward the freighter.

"Both of them caught her," Bacon said. "Almost immediately, she squatted down by the stern. When we surfaced a few minutes later, she wasn't in sight."

With her crew in high spirits as a result of their first successful attack, the American submarine pushed farther up into Davao Gulf. Around eight o'clock in the morning, she sighted another ship of about seven thousand tons. She was flying a battle flag—a red sun with red rays going out from it on a white background—which indicated that she was a naval auxiliary of some kind. Bacon maneuvered into position and fired three torpedoes. Two of them hit—one just forward of the bridge and the second right under it. The whole side of that Japanese ship fell in, or out. Bacon couldn't tell which it was. A cloud of brick-red smoke enveloped her from bow to stern.

At this unusual and unexpected sight, the submarine's skipper exclaimed: "Hey! Look at the red smoke coming up from the water!"

Signalman Hilbert, who was steering, replied, "Aw, Cap'n, that's just seven years of rust we're shaking down." All the officers and members of the crew were allowed to take a look at the stricken enemy. Even the men at the engines were relieved so they could look too. It was the first Japanese craft any of them actually had seen going under, and it was a soul-satisfying sight. Through the periscope, they watched Japanese soldiers running around wildly.

The auxiliary had three guns—bow, stern, and amidships—and they began firing. For a moment, the Americans thought the guns were firing at them, but they soon discovered that the panicky Japanese were firing on the opposite beam. Then the torpedoed ship settled in the bow and took a sharp list to port; she caught fire, and the submariners could see the men breaking out the fire hoses.

The enemy's fate was sealed. The Japanese apparently had been calling for help, as the *Pickerel* soon spotted planes coming out. She dove. The enemy aircraft dropped their bombs, and Prickett had his first experience with bombing in a submarine. "It was a doggone funny feeling," he said. "I can't describe it." As the submarine moved away, a couple of Japanese destroyers arrived on the scene and laid down depth charges, and Prickett had his first sample of ash-canning. "It was the same feeling—only worse," he said. But Bacon's craft was undamaged.

By this time, however, the Japanese had ample evidence that an aggressive American submarine was operating in the area. Their planes and destroyers made the vicinity decidedly uncomfortable. Along in the afternoon, the Americans came up for a look around. They could see ships along either side of the gulf from time to time, but they also observed a number of four-engined flying boats and three destroyers. The chances of getting into trouble were all too good. So Bacon headed the *Pickerel* out of the gulf and got clear of the enemy by evening.

The loyalty of the submarine crews to their skippers is intense, and with few exceptions the men in any given submarine are emphatic in declaring that they have the best captain in the service. Prickett described Bacon as one hundred per-cent perfect, quick-thinking and on the job every second. After the American ship had given the slip to the antisubmarine patrol in Davao Gulf, she ran into a rain squall that night. When the squall lifted, she'd run into something else. Prickett told about it.

They were on the surface. One of the lookouts suddenly called out:

"Ship on the starboard bow!"

Almost simultaneously, another lookout shouted:

"Ship on the port bow!"

Instantly Bacon yelled:

"Dive!"

As the men topside scrambled down the hatch, the submarine dove—fast! And none too soon. The crew could hear the roar of screws as two Japanese ships crossed above them from opposite directions. The first time over, the Japanese dropped no depth charges. Then they turned and started up what they believed was the submarine's track, letting go their ashcans. But they had figured incor-rectly; the Americans weren't there.

It had been a strenuous day and it wasn't over. Later, while Lieutenant Thomas F. Sharp, the gunnery officer, was officer of the deck, Bacon was lying down in the conning tower. Suddenly Sharp dove the ship.

"What have you got up there?" Bacon asked.

"Two destroyers," Sharp said.

"Do you think they saw us?"

The nerve-racking swish-boom of a depth charge answered the question. And more explosions followed quickly. The two Japanese warships were full of vinegar. They gave the submarine a heavy depth-charging and kept after her all that night and most of the morning. Not until about eleven o'clock were the American sub-mariners able to get out from under.

The *Pickerel* moved southward to the mouth of the Strait of Macassar, where there were signs that the Nipponese were preparing a big push. It didn't take Ba-con long to verify this. Late one afternoon he sighted a large convoy—cargo ships and destroyers, with a screen of planes. The submarine was too far off to get at it, but her skipper reported the presence of the enemy in large numbers—at least twelve ships seen and probably more beyond the horizon. Not long afterward another one of our submarines, on the basis of Bacon's report, was able to intercept them and make a successful attack.

Bacon took the *Pickerel* down off Balikpapan on Borneo, the third largest island in the world. There the water was glassy smooth and the weather hot, unfavorable for submarine operations. Besides, there were lots of destroyers and planes around, although this time they didn't all belong to the enemy. With great enjoyment, the Americans watched two Japanese destroyers take a beating from four United States Army bombers. The submarine was only about nine thousand yards away, and through the periscope her captain could see the Japanese weaving about at top speed, trying to avoid the bombs which were falling close to them.

The American submarine patrolled outside Balikpapan, where part of the convoy apparently had sought refuge, to pick off any of the Nipponese ships that might venture out. But none did; the Allied planes were too active. Signalman Way recalled that all that day the submarine's crew heard strange popping noises around their ship. They finally decided that what they heard were our bombs exploding at Balikpapan, forty or fifty miles away.

Because of the extreme heat, the *Pickerel*'s men usually went around dressed in skivvies and shoes, and tried to be as comfortable as possible. Only the lookouts put on a full array of clothing, and usually the officer of the deck was the only one in a uniform. When Prickett left Mariveles aboard the submarine he had a pair of Army brogans, but after the first depth-charging, the other men in the submarine ganged up on him and made him throw them away. They made too much noise. A pair of go-aheads obtained from a crewman took their place.

"Speaking of depth-charge attacks," Prickett said, "one time I was sitting in the dinette when they started up some of the auxiliary machinery. One of the pumps needed repairs and it sounded like a threshing machine. My nerves were so jumpy that when I heard it I thought it was a depth bomb right under me. I leaped over two tables before I realized what it was."

The *Pickerel* was ordered into Surabaya for an overhauling and refitting.

"When we reached the inside channel, we surfaced," Prickett said, "and it was the first time any of us had been in the sunshine in more than thirty days. The captain wouldn't let any of the crew stay topside for more than ten minutes. Even at that, some of them were pretty badly sunburned."

It was the last of January when Bacon's submarine pulled into the Netherlands naval base at Surabaya. She had been in service steadily since the outbreak of war and everyone aboard was nearly worn out. While the Dutch at the base took over and did their best to put the ship in condition, Bacon arranged for some rest camps for his officers and men.

"The only trouble, so far as I was concerned, was that I couldn't rest," he said. "I went to a hotel in the mountains, but my mind was so busy thinking things over, I couldn't sleep."

Three days later the Japanese started bombing, and the Americans had to rush back to their submarine and take her out and dive during the day. Although their stay ashore had been far from restful, the men were glad to shove off on patrol again. The *Pickerel's* course was through the Java Sea and by Macassar City, changing stations almost every night. At the end of February she was off Kupang, on Dutch Timor.

Bacon hadn't fired a torpedo on this patrol, and submarine skippers agree that lack of action is harder on submarine crews than almost anything else. After a few days with no attacks, the men begin to show signs of depression. Whether the enemy is sighted or not, constant vigilance must be maintained; the tension is always there and it gradually bears the crew down when it isn't broken by the stimulation and excitement of actual combat. Submariners want action.

Off Kupang, an enemy cruiser and destroyer showed up, although the Japanese at that time were making their landings on the opposite side of the big island. The cruiser stood off, and the next day her scout plane discovered the submarine. Bacon slipped away before the warship could get at him, but the destroyer came over and circled. The ship moved off without dropping any depth charges; later she returned and this time bore down on the submarine at full speed. When the *Pickerel* got underwater, the destroyer was only about eight hundred yards away. As she passed over, she dumped four depth charges.

"They were too close for comfort," Bacon said. "The explosions made the hatch bounce around and actually knocked the needles off some of the instruments."

They heard the destroyer pass over them again without dropping depth charges; a third time she came back and again laid down a pattern. For four hours she kept the submarine under, but Bacon finally got away.

The Battle of the Java Sea was shaping up, so the *Pickerel* went back there. It was a difficult spot for a submarine. Japanese destroyers were darting all around, and the Americans weren't able to get in a single attack. About this time the submarine *Perch*, a sister ship of the *Pickerel*, was sunk by the enemy. When last heard from, she was operating next to Bacon's ship. All through the war, the *Perch* was believed to have been lost with all hands, but after the Japanese surrender in Tokyo Bay, some of her officers and men were found in prison camps.

The Battle of the Java Sea was a defensive naval action, a desperate effort by American, British, Dutch and Australian warships to halt the oncoming Japanese. Although many of the enemy transports and warcraft were destroyed or damaged by our submarines and destroyers in the Java battle and preliminary actions, nevertheless we suffered our greatest defeat after Pearl Harbor.

It was a fight against heavy odds. As British Admiral Sir William James said, "Always there were too few ships; too few of everything."

All told, the United States lost the cruiser *Houston*, the carrier *Langley*, the destroyer *Pope* and the tanker *Pecos*. The Dutch lost two cruisers and two destroyers; the British lost one cruiser and four destroyers, and the Australian cruiser *Perth* was sent to the bottom. The cost to the Japanese was one cruiser and one destroyer, and a number of transports. In eight days, Japanese forces completed the seizure of the fabulously rich island of Java.

Bacon was ordered out of the Java Sea and headed for Fremantle, where he arrived March 19. The *Pickerel* was badly in need of overhauling again and the men aboard her were exhausted. They lay in port for three weeks, resting up and refitting the ship, and then shoved off.

Up to Cebu, in the Philippines, by way of Kupang and Macassar, the American submarine conducted an exploratory patrol. Although it was a long one both in time and in distance covered, it was primarily for reconnaissance purposes, and the *Pickerel* made only one attack. That was in Manipa Strait, in the Netherlands East Indies.

It was night when Bacon sighted a good-sized ship—a two-stacker—completely blacked out. The submarine made a good approach, with the target beautifully silhouetted against the moon. A spread of four torpedoes was fired from a range of about nine hundred yards. After a wait, the satisfying sound of an explosion drifted across the water as one of the missiles found its mark. The blast hardly had died away when a red glow appeared on the Japanese craft. She seemed to have caught fire. Then Bacon looked her over through his night glasses and immediately let out an exclamation of surprise and consternation.

After she had been hit, the blacked-out Nipponese craft had turned on an illuminated red cross on her side. There was something decidedly fishy about the situation. The Yanks moved closer for a better look. The ship, although hit, showed no indications of sinking. Bacon suspected a trick and decided to let well enough alone.

After taking a picture of the mysterious craft, he watched her drift off and then cleared the area. By this time Corregidor had fallen. The *Pickerel*, her scouting mission into the Philippines completed, returned to Fremantle. She had covered some eight thousand five hundred miles and spent fifty-one days at sea.

The area of the *Pickerel*'s last patrol under Bacon was to the east of the Philippines, in the Marianas Islands. She arrived in the vicinity of Guam without encountering any enemy ships that she could approach. Near Guam, however, she came across a large Japanese vessel. But the enemy craft was a beautiful white hospital ship with red crosses on her stack. The Americans looked her over and pulled away.

On Rota Island, north of Guam, however, Bacon located some game on which there was no closed season. Investigating a small bay, he surprised a 6,000-

ton freighter fast to a buoy and sent a torpedo crashing into her side. Almost at once fire broke out. It was well after sunset and the submarine wasn't able to see the target sink, but a few days later the Americans looked into the bay again. The ship had disappeared.

Pushing farther north to Saipan, they found some targets and made a few attacks, but without success. Then came orders to proceed to Pearl Harbor, and the weary submariners turned away from the war area. They had sunk enemy ships, they had performed valuable reconnaissance missions, but it had been drudgery and hard work, months of physical strain and nervous tension. The prospect of seeing Honolulu again was heartening, to say the least.

One of the most enjoyable diversions on their patrols had been listening to the radio. To the *Pickerel's* crew the propaganda of "Tokyo Rose," the Lady Haw-Haw of the Japanese, was funnier than any American comedy program. But their biggest kick came from the Manila radio, after the Japanese took it over and began to spread their propaganda on its waves.

For their theme song, opening and closing a government program, the Japanese used the stirring strains of John Philip Sousa's march "The Stars and Stripes Forever."

11 – Sixty Fathoms Deep

OVERHEAD JAPANESE SHIPS WERE passing back and forth—cruisers and destroyers, troopships and landing barges. Thousands of Japanese were swarming onto the beaches of northern Luzon. In time, they were to collide with the valiant American and Filipino fighters of MacArthur in the desperate Battle of Bataan; eventually, they were to capture The Rock, our fortress carved out of the island of Corregidor. With other thousands they would overrun most of the Philippines, but many of them were doomed to perish at the hands of the island's defenders.

Right now, however, the Japanese were hurrying to establish their first beachheads on the rich territory the warlords of Nippon had coveted for so many years. Inside an American submarine, lying motionless fifty feet deep in Lingayen Gulf, the men could hear the enemy ships clearly. They could distinguish the rumbling of the transport propellers and the faster churning of the screws of the destroyers. They didn't need a listening device to catch these harrowing sounds. Besides, the growl of the enemy propellers was almost the only sound that came to the Americans down there under the water.

It was deathly quiet inside the steel hull of the submarine. Although the air wasn't actually cold, it had a clammy quality that seemed to chill the bones of the anxiously listening crew. Everything was shut down except the sound gear. The men moved about, when it was absolutely necessary for them to move at all, in bare or stockinged feet. The few commands from the officers were uttered in whispers.

The submarine was an old-timer, one of our S-boats—the *S-38*. The war was scarcely two weeks old, but already she had sunk a Japanese cargo ship. She was on the point of sinking more enemy craft when she had run aground. Instead of punching torpedoes into warships, she was lying on the bottom of Lingayen Gulf with her nose shoved deep in the muck.

Up above in the warm Philippine sunlight, Japanese ships continued to move back and forth. In the black water below, the crew of the S-boat waited and hoped, and more than a few of the men silently prayed.

At his station at the listening gear was a radioman first class, a lean-faced young fellow of average height but well set up. If any of his companions had asked for a prayer to repeat, he could have supplied it promptly; his father had been a Methodist minister, and his years until he completed high school had been spent in a household where praying was the order of the day. He was John Morgan McNeal, born in Evergreen, Alabama. The reports he made, which enabled the captain to form some sort of picture of the scene above, were in the accent of the South.

In the Navy, you usually have to rate what you get. When you make it the hard way, up from green "boots" to gold braid, you've proved yourself a good man.

McNeal, fourteen years in the Navy, was in the course of demonstrating that, even in the most rugged arm of the service, the submarines.

When young John McNeal joined the Navy in 1927, after his graduation from high school in Auburn, Alabama, it wasn't with the idea of serving a hitch or two for the excitement and adventure. He had made up his mind that the Navy would be his career. He had lived and gone to school in numerous towns in Alabama and Florida as his father had been transferred to different churches. His high school education began at Pensacola, Florida, and ended at Auburn, where he won his letters in football, baseball, basketball, and track. McNeal had "been around," and knew what he wanted.

After basic training at Norfolk, Virginia, he passed the test for radio school; completing that, he was transferred to the submarine base at New London, Connecticut, and assigned to his first submarine, the *S-11*, on December 11, 1928. A month later, he was off for Coco Solo, Canal Zone. Six months later, he was advanced to radioman third class. All told, he had served in five submarines and had been advanced to radioman first class when he joined the *S-38*, in December 1939.

So far, his story had been one of slow but steady advancement by an enlisted man who loved the Navy and was determined to get ahead in the service. The war was to step up the tempo of his progress.

The *S-38* was on patrol when the war broke.

"We were not surprised when it came," McNeal said. "But still we were all keyed up. First thing, of course, we got busy and made ready the fire stores—put warheads on the torpedoes and so on. Our first orders were to patrol Calavite Pass."

For several days, the *S-38* hunted in the Cape Calavite area, about a hundred miles south of the entrance to Manila Bay, without sighting any enemy craft. About the fourth night, while she was cruising on the surface, the lookout spotted a blur that gradually sharpened into the outlines of a medium-sized freighter. Excitement swept the crew, eager to draw their first blood. They took their battle stations, battle stations that for the first time in the experience of any of them meant business.

The submarine's captain, Lieutenant Commander W. G. ("Moon") Chapple, coolly determined to start off his part in the war with a bang. He was taking no chances of a miss on this, his first, attack and luck was with him. Against the background of the land shadow, the *S-38* was invisible to the enemy, while the target was silhouetted against the sky for those topside. Chapple started his approach, proceeding cautiously until his submarine was only about two thousand yards from the freighter.

Came the order: "Fire one!"

The S-boat quivered as the torpedo slipped from its tube and sliced through the night waters of the pass toward the enemy cargo ship. Then the tense wait ...

It was perfect!

Thunder rolled across the pass to the Americans. The torpedo's explosion virtually split the enemy vessel in two. Even while the jubilant group on the bridge watched, the ship settled lower and lower, and in less than a minute slid beneath the surface.

That, however, was the last enemy ship the S-boat encountered in the area, and on December 21 Chapple's submarine was ordered to Lingayen Gulf, where the Japanese were expected to make landings. The *S-38* arrived outside the entrance to the gulf during the night and, submerging just before dawn, went on in about six o'clock in the morning. Through the periscope, her captain soon saw that the Japanese were indeed preparing to put troops ashore.

He sighted two transports and several destroyers escorting them.

Here was something worthwhile, and the *S-38* began an approach on the transports. The enemy destroyers, however, discovered her before she was in position to launch her torpedoes. They tore after her and while she was eluding them, a thumping good depth-charging shook her up.

The Americans nevertheless continued to prowl around the inner shore of the gulf, looking for new prey. Most of the time the *S-38* was completely submerged; her skipper contented himself with quick peeks through the periscope.

Then it happened—about ten o'clock in the morning. There was a trembling through the hull from bow to stern. The submarine moved crazily ahead a few feet and stopped dead. She lay in the ooze of the gulf's bottom, only fifty feet down. And before she could extricate herself, the enemy's cruisers and destroyers, troopships and landing barges began to pass back and forth overhead.

The unlucky American submariners were consoled by only two small facts: the enemy surface ships were not aware that she was lying beneath them, and no planes were overhead to spot her shadowy outline in the depths. But Moon Chapple and his men had no means of knowing how long that state of affairs would continue. "For twelve hours," McNeal said, "we lay on bottom, listening to those Jap ships moving around above us. It was a long twelve hours, believe me. But toward the end of the day things quieted down. Finally, at ten that night, we started backing out of the mud."

This was a hazardous job. One of the submarine's screws was badly bent and set up enough vibration and noise to shatter almost any listening gear that might be in the vicinity. But it was get out or good-bye for the Yanks. They gave their ship all she had, until at last she eased astern and pulled free of the muck that had gripped her.

In the sheltering darkness, the *S-38* surfaced and moved across the gulf. During the night she watched a couple of Japanese destroyers on patrol, but couldn't get a shot at them. At dawn she dove and again spent the day on bottom. That night she charged her batteries and, crippled though she was, doggedly headed back across the gulf the next morning. Things were good and lively by this time. Troopships loaded to the rails with Japanese soldiers were arriving steadily. Captain Chappie's periscope showed him about thirty transports of all sizes, with escort destroyers skittering around them. This was good hunting—almost too good.

But, undaunted, the submarine began to stalk the transport fleet. She was maneuvering into position to fire, and it looked more and more likely that she would plant a few torpedoes in Japanese hulls, when a loud blast on her starboard side rocked her violently. The crew were not sure what the explosion came from, but decided it had been an aerial bomb. There was no doubt that their presence had been discovered. Crisscrossing destroyers began weaving a pattern of depth bombs over that section of Lingayen Gulf. The *S-38* got out of there as fast as she could. Late that night she eased up to the surface well out in the gulf. She had only three torpedoes, one screw was badly damaged. The waters on all sides were alive with enemy warcraft. And then, as the battery blower was started, there was an explosion within the hull of the submarine itself.

The noise of the blast scarcely had died out when through the ship screamed the fire-collision alarm, a shrill siren. The men raced to their stations. Fires appeared in several places, and smoke billowed out of the after-battery room. Desperately, but with well-trained efficiency, the crew attacked this newest peril. They opened the engine-room hatch to get the smoke out. Coughing and choking in the fumes, they fought the flames. It was for this moment they had gone through their fire drill numberless times.

And they licked the blazing enemy. Then they cleared away the after battery where the explosion had occurred and checked the damage.

Three men had been injured, two seriously. Only the forward battery now was available for maneuvering submerged, and it was badly run down. The submarine was highly vulnerable, with a bent screw and little juice in her one usable battery, as she started ahead on the surface in an attempt to sneak through the entrance of the gulf. She had proceeded only a short distance when through the gloom the lookout sighted a pair of Japanese destroyers.

It was Christmas Eve.

Almost as soon as the *S-38* discovered the two enemy warcraft, they wheeled and headed for her at top speed. With her one usable battery almost exhausted, Chappie's submarine made a quick dive, barely in time. The Japanese were snapping at her heels and as they churned above her, they dumped a series of depth charges. Apparently the destroyers thought they were so close that their ashcans couldn't fail to eliminate the submarine, because that was all the blasting they gave her.

The explosions were terrific, and the luckless S-boat shivered from end to end. Cork and paint showered down on the sprawling crew. For a few moments, most of them were convinced that this was the end. But the sturdy undersea fighter shook herself and intact, but a little groggy, started crawling under the ocean toward Mariveles.

She struggled out beyond the gulf and into the South China Sea, and promptly ran into more trouble. Japanese destroyers in considerable numbers were patrolling the area.

There seemed to be only one thing to do—find a comfortable submerged ledge and sit on it until the waters above were free of enemy warcraft. Chappie managed to locate a suitable ledge and eased his ship onto it. He drew a long sigh of relief. At last it began to look as if their luck had taken a turn for the better. Then the S-boat began to slip. Before her crew could do anything about it, she had toppled off her perch and was plunging toward the bottom of the sea.

Her diving officer fought frantically to catch her, but the terrifying descent continued. Down and down she dropped. Within one minute, the gauges showed she had reached a depth of sixty fathoms—three hundred and sixty feet.

The *S-38* was a veteran of World War I. She had never been designed to withstand the crushing pressure of such an ocean depth. Yet, in tribute to the skillful designing and honest workmanship that had gone into her more than two decades before, she did withstand it. And at three hundred and sixty feet, the diving officer stopped her drop. He blew all her tanks; she came up in a hurry and burst forth onto the surface of the sea.

There wasn't a Japanese warship in sight! For a couple of hours, the submarine remained on the surface, charging her one good battery. After that, she dove and started to limp toward home. Chappie and his men spent Christmas Day striving desperately to reach a haven, and when they finally came in sight of Mariveles, it was all the Christmas present any of them could have hoped for.

The *S-38* snuggled up alongside the submarine tender *Canopus*. The three injured men were transferred to her. Then the crews of both ships began repairs on the after battery, and loaded torpedoes and supplies aboard. It took several days to recondition the submarine, because work could be carried on only at night, since the *S-38* had to submerge by day to avoid Japanese bombs.

Meanwhile, Chapple took an extra officer and several men on board just as Lieutenant Commander Bacon of the *Pickerel* was doing at the same time. McNeal managed to get one of his friends on the S-boat, a radioman first class named Barney Barnum, who had served on the ship before.

On New Year's Day, the Chapple submarine shoved off for Surabaya, Java. The ship was in bad shape and had orders to make no attacks on the way. She arrived at the Dutch naval base in the early part of January and was immediately put into drydock, while half her crew was sent to resorts in the mountains to rest, McNeal among them. At Surabaya, Chapple left the *S-38* and was assigned to another submarine. Lieutenant Hank Munson took over as captain.

Munson's first patrol area was off Balikpapan, which was fast becoming the hot corner of the Netherlands East Indies. The Dutchmen at Surabaya had done a good job on the overhaul of the submarine, according to McNeal, and the Americans were primed for action. They found it the first night in the area—but they were on the receiving end. A pair of enemy destroyers got on their tail.

"They had a couple of the smartest soundmen I've ever encountered," McNeal said. "They kept their ships right on top of us, and we took a good working over before we got away."

For about two weeks, the submarine prowled around Macassar Strait and then, not having had any luck, she moved down to Surabaya again, where she spent four days. When she left Surabaya, the *S-38* landed right in the middle of the Battle of the Java Sea. Nipponese warships were everywhere, and on the lookout for submarines. Not a day went by that Munson's S-boat didn't dodge enemy depth-charge attacks. But Munson had his innings too, and on one occasion fired two torpedoes at a light cruiser and one at a destroyer that was accompanying her. The submariners heard explosions, but it was no time to view results through a periscope. They felt pretty certain nevertheless that they had badly damaged or sunk the cruiser and might have blasted the destroyer.

The night after the battle, the Yankee submarine was on the surface, charging her batteries. With enemy warships roaming the Java Sea, this operation called for the greatest vigilance. The lookouts strained their eyes to pierce the surrounding darkness; they tuned their ears to catch the faintest unusual sound. About two o'clock, one of them called down that he believed he had heard faint cries for help. A moment later he announced that he was certain of it.

Captain Munson headed the *S-38* in the direction from which the cries seemed to come. Cautiously she eased ahead. She was in enemy waters, and the Japanese had shown they would try anything to catch our submarines in booby traps. One of the group on the bridge suddenly picked up a bobbing pinpoint of light—then a second, and a third. All those topside soon could see them, and as the submarine pulled nearer, they could distinguish the dim outlines of several life rafts against the black water.

Soon shouts were exchanged between the submarine's skipper and the men on the rafts. One thing was certain. The men out there in the darkness were not Japanese. Their accents were as English as Yorkshire pudding. Munson maneuvered close to the rafts and one by one the men on them were pulled aboard; fifty-six passed through the hatch and into the submarine. It was a long and arduous job. Some of the men on the rafts were badly injured, just barely alive. To pass these men through the twenty-three-inch hatchway, down the iron ladders into the belly of the ship called for painstaking care. Many of them had gaping shrapnel wounds; others were seriously burned.

When the last man had been saved from the sea, the rafts were set adrift, and the submariners started looking after their many passengers.

"I helped carry one British sailor through the forward battery door," McNeal said. "The poor fellow's back was shot full of holes. We laid him on a bunk and gave him a shot of whisky. It seemed to pick him up for a moment, and he tried to talk. Then he sank back—and that was the end."

The rescued sailors were from HMS *Electra*, a destroyer which the British lost in the Java Sea battle. Among the survivors was the ship's surgeon who, fortunately, was uninjured. The *S-38* crew located some catgut and with this the *Electra*'s doctor performed heroic service sewing up wounds.

With about one hundred men aboard, Munson's submarine headed straight for Surabaya. It took her twenty-four hours to reach port, hours no one on the ship ever will forget. The submarine was filled with the moans of wounded men, and there was hardly enough room for those operating the ship to turn around in.

As the *S-38* moved into the channel at Surabaya, she saw HMS *Exeter* pulling out. The gallant British cruiser steamed forth into the Java Sea and the end of her glorious career. With almost no ammunition left, she tried to flee and failed. When the Americans left the rescued British at Surabaya, they gave them most of their blankets and all the clothing they could possibly spare.

The run into Fremantle was uneventful.

"When we reached Fremantle we got a nice liberty and a royal reception," McNeal said. "Everybody we met greeted us with 'Glad to see you, Yanks'." He smiled a little as he told about it. "I'm from way down South, but that was one time I didn't mind being called a Yank."

At Fremantle, McNeal was advanced to chief radioman.

"We worked on our ship and got it in good shape," he said. "Then we got underway for the east coast of Australia. Our first stop was at Melbourne, where we got liberty and had a good time. Those Australians were certainly nice to us. After that we put in at Brisbane."

Munson's submarine lay in Brisbane ten days and then was ordered to Port Moresby, on the southern coast of Papua. She patrolled this area for a while without any encounters with the enemy. After that she moved eastward into the Coral Sea. It was the early part of May, and seventy miles north of her the Battle of the Coral Sea was taking place. This was our first naval victory and it saved Australia from the Japanese. But Munson's submarine was unable to get in any punches. She had a rough trip and took a few blows from the wind and water that tore away about half of her after superstructure. At the end of a month she was back in Brisbane.

The *S-38*'s score against the enemy up to that time, so far as her crew were able to ascertain, was five vessels sunk. McNeal was ordered back to the United States. When he arrived in New York the first part of July he found a pleasant surprise. It was his commission as an ensign, dated June 15.

"I had been hoping and half expecting that I might be promoted," he said, "but jumping warrant and chief warrant officer was more than I had dreamed of." McNeal had gone up the hard way, and he knew his stuff.

12 – They Used to be Pig-Boats

THE TERM "PIG-BOAT" AS APPLIED TO submarines does not stem, as many people seem to believe, from the conditions that existed aboard these craft back in the old days, nor from the grimy and disheveled appearance of the hardy men who manned them.

To hear veterans describe these early submarines, however, one concludes that "pig-boat" was a very fitting name. Until the E-boats, there were no bunks aboard. Crews and officers alike stretched out on the greasy steel deck. And until the D-boats appeared, the toilet was a bucket.

Pictures of our submarine crews taken more than thirty years ago, as they lined up topside of their "diving coffins," show groups which generally look more like a shift of miners emerging from a coal pit than a group of sailors.

Obviously there was no room below decks to shave. Even the kindly grays and blacks of the photographic plate could not conceal their rumpled clothing, which was as grease smeared as that of a driller on a flowing oil well. This is no cause for wonder. The early diesels were cantankerous, and much of the time was devoted to pulling them apart and putting the pieces back together again. The open batteries kept the electricians on the jump trying to make them charge and discharge without blowing up the ship. The gunners' mates spent many long hours trying to master the eccentricities of the early torpedoes.

Nevertheless, the name "pig-boats" came to be applied to the submarines for another reason. In those early days, a division of half a dozen submarines was almost invariably accompanied by a tender. Generally the tender was a single-turret monitor which had outgrown its usefulness as a fighting craft and had been demoted to nursing a flock of the Navy's newest experimental ships. And the submarines were well tied to the apron strings of the mothership. She hovered around anxiously when they dove at sea. Safe in port, the division would huddle about her, made fast alongside.

One day a Navy man, whose name is not known, noticed a division of submarines cuddled up to a mothership. Being a farm boy, he recognized with a touch of homesickness that the round-bellied little submarines looked very much like a litter of suckling pigs squealing up to a mother sow at mealtime.

He commented on this, and the name "pig-boat" was born.

The submarine itself was born long before. The recorded history of man shows numerous instances of his efforts to navigate underwater, just as it includes many examples of his attempts to fly. Alexander the Great, legend has it, was an early submariner. He is said to have sat in a "watertight bell and defied the whale." Why the young conqueror was so defiant is not recorded—perhaps he just wished to show the whale that he too could probe the watery depths.

Even before Alexander, however, the inventive Greeks used some sort of diving bell. It was during the siege of Troy, Aristotle relates, but since he doesn't elaborate, the device must not have been completely successful.

Although it is hard to believe that no one made any further effort to navigate underwater for many hundreds of years, the records suggest nothing until about the sixteenth century, when there appears to have been quite a flurry of interest in the subject. In Spain, in Italy, and in the Low Countries, ambitious inventors put forward various designs for submersibles. Even Leonardo da Vinci, willing to try anything, took a whirl at it. Most of the devices were either the diving-bell type or explosive carriers. They had one thing in common: they didn't work. In the seventeenth century, however, the submarine inventors began to get somewhere—under the water and back to the surface, alive and breathing. In 1620, Cornelius van Drebbel, a Dutchman, built an underwater rowboat that worked fairly well—so well, in fact, that four years later his patron, King James I of England, took a ride in it. Van Drebbel's submarine was made waterproof with oiled leather. It could remain submerged for several hours, propelled about by oars, with its air revitalized by some secret method which the inventor never imparted to anyone. The Dutch inventor deserves the credit for constructing the first submarine successfully to carry human beings underwater.

In 1652, a Frenchman designed and built a veritable giant of a submarine: seventy-two feet long and twelve feet wide which was called the "Rotterdam Boat." It was pushed through the water by means of a pair of paddles, operated by hand. The inventor thoughtfully provided his strange craft with a set of legs so that it could squat on the river bottom and give the paddle turners a chance to catch their breath now and then. There followed a number of other, and less successful, attempts at submarine building in Italy and England. Then during the American Revolution, a Connecticut man constructed a weird contraption that was the first of its kind to sink a ship in time of war. He was David Bushnell, a native of Saybrook.

British warships were raising havoc along the New England coast, bombarding towns and sinking or seizing colonial shipping. Bushnell, his ire aroused, decided to do something about it. First he demonstrated that gunpowder could be exploded underwater. Next he turned his talents to making a machine which would plant the charges of gunpowder where they would bring the desired result—destroy King George's men-of-war. The outcome was the American *Turtle*, which Bushnell built at Saybrook. It was made of oak and derived its name from the fact that its hull was composed of two shells vaguely resembling turtle shells.

The *Turtle* was operated by one man, who pumped a screw propeller. Water for ballast came in through a valve in the bottom and was pushed out again by hand pumps. There was enough air inside to keep the operator going about half an hour. Benjamin Franklin himself suggested the use of phosphorus for its lighting system. An oak bomb filled with one hundred and fifty pounds of gunpowder, which was exploded by a time device, was carried above the *Turtle*'s rudder. With a Sergeant Lee as its one-man crew, Bushnell's submarine went into action in New York Harbor in April 1777. By night, Lee pedaled the *Turtle* under Lord Howe's Eagle, a sixty-four-gun ship. Then he ran into trouble. He tried to screw his wooden bomb to the victim, but he was under a metal part of the hull and the screws wouldn't hold. He left the bomb and took his submarine away to safety. In due time the bomb exploded; it failed to damage the vessel because it had drifted too far away, but it scared the wits out of the crew.

The *Turtle*'s next attack was on the Cerberus, anchored off New London. Again the wooden bomb failed to stick to the hull. As it floated away, however, three curious sailors on board a captured schooner which the Cerberus had in tow hauled it aboard. The powder was set off in time, and that was the end of both schooner and crew—the first victims of a submarine attack. Later, Bushnell built a number of mines, similar to the *Turtle* in shape, but without crews. They were cast into the Delaware River just above Philadelphia, whence they drifted down among a fleet of British ships. When they began to explode they sank a small schooner, and the British hurriedly withdrew.

Every schoolboy knows that Robert Fulton is credited with being the inventor of the steamboat, but few people know that long before the steamboat, Fulton designed and built a successful submarine. About the turn of the nineteenth century, while Fulton was an art student in Paris, he conceived the idea of his underwater boat, which he later built and named the *Nautilus*. Jules Verne, when he wrote his *Twenty Thousand Leagues Under the Sea*, used the name of Fulton's craft for his fictional submarine. Our Navy, too, named one of our biggest undersea fighters that sank Japanese ships the *Nautilus*.

Fulton's submarine had a number of novel features. It was about six feet in diameter and more nearly resembled a modern submarine in shape than had most of its predecessors. It had reservoirs of compressed air for breathing, and it submerged and surfaced by means of water ballast tanks. It also was equipped with horizontal planes. Probably its most unusual feature was a set of sails—these could be furled, and the mast struck in time for the ship to get below surface within a couple of minutes.

Fulton also developed underwater mines and torpedoes for use by the *Nautilus*. He offered the whole outfit to his government, which promptly turned it down. He finally took his invention to England, and in 1805 he showed the British what it could do. Making an underwater approach in true modern style, he blew up a 200-ton brig with 170 pounds of gunpowder.

It was a convincing demonstration, but the British naval officers refused to be persuaded and declared that Fulton's craft was impracticable. Had he been able to foresee what would happen a little more than a century later, Fulton undoubtedly would have said to these men, "You'll be sorry!"

As it was, the discouraged inventor packed up and went home. A couple of years later he prevailed on this government to sponsor his experiments. He blew up a brig with a torpedo in another successful demonstration, but more obstacles and discouragements were piled in his way until at last, fed up with red tape and political rigmarole, Fulton turned to steamboats.

Men who believed that they could solve the problems of underwater navigation became more numerous as the century grew older. An American named Mix, an Englishman named Captain Johnson, a German named Bauer, a Frenchman named Le Brun, and a Spaniard named Monturiol constructed submarines of one sort or another. It was a contest of all nations. Le Brun's ship, the *Plongeur*, was unusual in that it was propelled by compressed air. In the Civil War, the Confederate States turned to underwater craft in the hope of nullifying the Union Navy, and achieved some startling, if discouraging, results.

The Confederacy built three submarines and a number of craft known as Davids, after David who slew Goliath, which were semisubmersible. In 1862 the privately financed *Pioneer* was built and presented to the Confederacy. She was twenty feet long and constructed of quarter-inch sheet iron, with bow and stern rudders and side vanes. Two men supplied the power for her propeller. After successful trials, which included blowing up a target barge, the *Pioneer* was considered ready to meet the enemy.

Admiral Farragut moved up the Mississippi to capture New Orleans, and the Confederate submarine bravely set forth to halt him. But something went wrong. She got out of control and ended her career ingloriously by sinking in the river with all her crew.

The South's second submarine sank before it even completed its trial. And then came the *Hunley*, soon to be known as the "Peripatetic Coffin." The theory of the *Hunley*'s operation was to tow a torpedo on a 200-foot line, dive under the intended victim, and come to the surface after the explosion. Like many plausible ideas in connection with submarines, it had one grievous fault—it didn't work. As a matter of fact, the *Hunley* herself didn't work.

On a trial run she dove to the bottom of Mobile Bay and stayed there until all on board, an officer and eight men, suffocated. But the Southerners were game. They raised her, and nine volunteers tried her out in Charleston. They met the same fate. All told, the *Hunley* disposed of five crews in this fashion. The Confederates were convinced; they decided, after hauling her to the surface for the fifth time, to convert her into a David. In the Davids, steam engines furnished the power, so they had to have funnels. That meant they couldn't submerge completely, but ran with their decks awash, and when attacking drew in their funnels almost level with the water.

With the exception of the converted *Hunley*, none of them sank any ships. The first of the Davids did, however, damage a Union ironclad. They all carried sixty pounds of gunpowder in copper torpedoes at the end of twenty-two-foot booms attached to their bows. The *Hunley*, in the role of a David, wound up her career in a blaze of glory. On the night of February 17, 1864, she sneaked up on the USS *Housatonic*, lying in the north channel at Charleston. When the noise and smoke and general confusion had cleared away, the *Housatonic* was sunk and the *Hunley* and her crew blown to pieces. During the last half of the nineteenth century, there were hundreds of experimenters in undersea craft on both sides of the ocean. Several developments of great importance were made: the invention of the Whitehead torpedo in England in 1864; it was the first compressed-air driven torpedo; the construction of an all-steel submarine in France; and one, built by Romazzotti, a Frenchman – a submarine with a double hull

Our Navy wasn't very interested in these goings on. Its attitude was expressed by one high official, who said that "no one but a crazy man would waste his time inventing a submarine, and no one but another lunatic would go down in it if it were invented." But during the second administration of Grover Cleveland, when we got into an argument with Britain over the Venezuela boundary line, Congress discovered that our Navy had sunk into "innocuous desuetude." Stricken with jitters, the lawmakers on Capitol Hill surprised everybody by including in their naval appropriations $200,000 with which to build experimental submarines.

The Navy had the money, but its secretary, Hilary A. Herbert, was skeptical. He doubted that life could endure in a submerged vessel if an explosion took place anywhere near it, and he hesitated to order the use of the fund in a way that might jeopardize human lives unduly. This resulted in our Navy's achieving a "first" in one phase of submarine warfare. It made the first depth-charge attack.

Inside a watertight tank were put a cat, a rooster, a rabbit and a dove. Then the tank was submerged and set adrift, and a series of underwater explosions of guncotton were touched off at varying distances from it, the closest about one hundred feet away. When the tank was hauled out of the water and opened up, it was found that the rabbit and the dove hadn't survived these depth charges, but the cat and the rooster were alive.

The Secretary of the Navy was satisfied; a call for bids on a submarine was issued in 1895. Eight different inventors made bids; two of them, Simon Lake and John P. Holland, were destined to play an important part in submarine history.

For some reason Lake never received a contract from this government, but he built a number of submarines for other countries. Probably his greatest contribution to the modern submarine was the development of the "level-keel" as compared to the "diving" type. He also introduced the use of two sets of hydroplanes for helping to maintain a ship at the desired depth, a method of control used today. Holland, however, was given the Navy contract. The history of his interest in submarines was a strange one. As a young man, he had fled from Ireland to the United States, bringing with him an intense dislike for England. He was determined to contribute his share toward the freeing of Ireland by rendering the British Navy powerless through submarines. He conceived this plan as early as his seventeenth year, but not until he was thirty-five, in 1877, did he launch his first successful underwater boat in New Jersey's Passaic River.

Shaped like a cigar, the original *Holland* was ten feet long and required a crew of one. Motive power came from a steam boiler made of a beer keg, which was carried on a launch trailing behind. The ship not only ran on the surface but made some short dives and once stayed underwater for twenty-four hours with its intrepid inventor inside it.

Holland's first submarine had been financed by fellow Irish patriots; its performance evidently pleased them, because they produced $13,000 more with which Holland built his second submersible, named the *Fenian Ram*. It was thirty feet long, weighed seventeen tons, and had an engine that wouldn't work. It took two years to build this submarine, and before the balky engine could be fixed Holland's backers got into a quarrel among themselves, and someone stole the *Fenian Ram*. That was that. Holland built another submarine, in co-operation with Edward Zalinski, an Army officer who was attempting to develop a torpedo gun. This craft, however, was irreparably damaged in the launching.

The Irish inventor's fourth submarine was the one built for the Navy at a price of $150,000. This was the *Plunger*. It had two torpedo tubes, was eighty-five feet long, and displaced one hundred sixty-eight tons. The Navy's engineers, however, put their oar in and demanded that a certain type of steam engine be installed. When the *Plunger* fired up, she became so hot inside that no one could have lived in her, and she was never tested.

Holland was neither surprised nor discouraged. He made a deal with the Navy to build another submarine without any interference. The result was the *Holland*, the first ship of the United States Submarine Service. Her keel was laid down in 1898, although the Navy did not approve the craft and pay the $150,000 purchase price until two years later. Incidentally, she was a bargain because it cost *Holland*'s company about $250,000 to build her. By more modern standards, the *Holland* was a tiny ship—fifty-four feet long, with a submerged displacement of seventy-three tons and a cruising radius of some two hundred miles. She had a single torpedo tube and could chug along at six knots on the surface and almost as fast when submerged. She was driven on the surface by a fifty-horsepower gasoline engine, and by electric motors when submerged. On April 18, 1900, *Holland* was paid for his craft and the Navy entered the submarine field.

In spite of her small size, the *Holland* made a deep impression on the Navy and for a long time our submarines were frequently referred to as 'Hollands.' *Holland*'s company not only received an order for six more improved submarines, but also started Japan's submarine fleet by selling her five boats in 1900. The company disposed of five boats to Britain the next year, and still later sold some to Russia.

In the more than forty-five years since the United States got the first *Holland*, our submarines have gone forward a long way. The modern fleet submarines built during the war and in the years just preceding are from three hundred to three hundred twenty feet long and have a displacement of about fifteen hundred tons on the surface. The earlier ones cost $5,500,000 but before the war this had gone up another two million dollars. These new-type submarines have a cruising range in excess of twelve thousand miles and their torpedoes a range of more than nine thousand yards.

On an average, they carry eighty-five officers and men. A few years after World War I, the United States built three much larger submarines, but experience proved that they were less effective than the smaller ships. These big submarines were in the Argonaut class. The *Argonaut* herself was three hundred seventy feet long, with a surface displacement of two thousand seven hundred tons and carried a personnel of eighty-eight men. She was sunk during the war in a battle with Japanese destroyers in the Southwest Pacific. The other two submarines in this class were the *Narwhal* and the *Nautilus*, both a little smaller than the *Argonaut*.

In the early submarines all the enlisted men were petty officers, as most of them are today. Until after World War I each new submarine design was given a letter of the alphabet. In the E-boats, there were only three ratings aboard—gunners' mates, machinists' mates and electricians, later changed to electricians' mates. The storage batteries were wide open, and explosions were frequent. The Navy was lucky, however, and very few men lost their lives in these blasts until the *E-2*, while testing the Edison battery, had an explosion that killed fourteen men. Except for some experimental G-boats, the Ds were the last of the gasoline submarines. The Es were the first of the diesels. One of the big disadvantages of the gas-driven craft was that the fumes frequently would make the crew "goofy." When any of the men began to giggle and laugh, the captain knew it was time to get them out in the air in a hurry. Admiral Withers recalls pulling nine unconscious men out of a boat, when they were overcome by the fumes, and working long and hard to bring them to.

It would be difficult to exaggerate what a dauntless personnel these pig-boats had. On one occasion the *E-1*, with Withers in command, was off Pensacola. It was windy and rough and growing late. The E-boat signaled the tender, a single-turret monitor, to give her a tow. Those monitors had so little freeboard that in rough weather they almost looked like submarines themselves. They wouldn't steer within twenty-five degrees of a course, but they'd come out and pick up a submarine in any old kind of blow.

The *E-1*'s mothership approached the bobbing submarine and shot a line from a gun. It whizzed over it at high speed, narrowly missing the men on the ship's tiny bridge. The E-boat's captain shouted for them not to try that again. He'd come over. The submarine maneuvered close to the tender and picked up the line, but it went under the rudder and they had to let it go. The next time it carried away the submarine's towing pennant. After several more failures, the E-boat went right alongside the tender, and the line was passed to them.

Having lost her towing pennant, Withers' pig-boat was faced with the problem of making fast the towline. It was growing steadily rougher, and the submarine was rolling violently, with the sea breaking over her. One of the ratings named Elmore volunteered to take the line up to the bow and fasten it onto the pelican hook. He inched his way forward and after some difficulty managed to make it fast. Just then the submarine's nose went under. When it came up again—there was no Elmore.

Somebody shouted, "Man overboard!"

From the monitor, a life buoy came hurtling through the air, and as it hit the water, its flares lit up the fast-gathering darkness. Another big wave drove the submarine's bow under again. When it came up—there was Elmore! Not only that, there was the sputtering smoky life buoy on the E-1's quarter-deck. By the time Elmore had crawled on hands and knees back to the conning tower and, wet but safe, disappeared down the hatch, the tender had forged ahead at full speed into the wind. She went ahead so fast she jerked the submarine into the sea. The water smashed the bridge, and from then on the two officers had to stand watch in the conning tower, not unlike a steel hogshead, and peer out through a porthole the size of a stove lid.

"Just before it got dark," Admiral Withers recalls, "I took a bearing on a lighthouse. All that night we bounced around on the end of the towline. When morning came we saw another lighthouse, and I figured it was the next one down the coast, about thirty miles. But it was the same lighthouse I'd taken the bearing on the night before. The tender had been towing us into the wind all night, and we'd gone nowhere."

Probably the most remarkable exploit of the many performed by the E-1's crew was that of a rather smallish gunner's mate named Kuhn. The pig-boat was on torpedo practice. It fired a torpedo, but the starting mechanism failed to trip, and the torpedo plunked right down to the bottom of the ocean. The submarine had little difficulty in locating it. It was the ingenious custom to have the torpedoes leak a little air for just such a contingency. Bubbles rising to the surface indicated its position.

The E-1's lost "pickle" was in ninety feet of water. Kuhn was put into a diving suit and sent down to hook lines onto it. Even though the torpedoes of those days were only eighteen inches in diameter as compared with the twenty-one inches of today and considerably shorter, they nevertheless cost too much to lose without a struggle. Soon from the ocean's floor came the signal to haul up the diving gunner's mate. The men on the submarine noticed that he was pretty heavy, but they pulled away with a will, and in a few minutes his diminutive figure broke the surface.

That wasn't all. Kuhn's arms and legs were tightly wound about the lost torpedo. If, by any chance, he had tripped the starting mechanism on his way up, he would have been ground to hamburger. Man and torpedo were dragged aboard the submarine.

"What was the idea of bringing that torpedo up with you?" Withers demanded.

"Well, Cap'n," Kuhn said apologetically, "it was like this. When I got down there I found the torpedo all right, but I couldn't hook my lines onto it. I'd lost them. I didn't want to have to come down again, so I just carried it up with me."

The Japanese Bombing of Darwin, Australia, 19 February 1942

13 - "This is Not a Drill."

ANY WAY YOU LOOK AT IT, submariners do not relish the thought of bombers overhead. To be sure, a submarine presents a slender, difficult target on the surface of the sea, and given only a slight head start can find safety by diving. But it has no adequate arms with which to fight off the sky attackers, and its relatively thin steel skin is not meant to withstand aerial bombs. There is only one answer for a submarine: don't get hit.

Thus our submarines patrolling near Pearl Harbor found themselves in a very difficult situation when the Commander in Chief of the Pacific Fleet sent out the radio message which brought American ships into action all over the western ocean. The message itself, in Navy fashion, was simple and to the point; its implications staggered the imagination. Decoded, it read: "Pearl Harbor being bombed. This is not a drill."

Soon after receiving this message, one of our Pearl Harbor submarines found herself in an especially hot spot, one that had all the elements of comedy but nevertheless might wind up in tragedy. She was returning from patrol, but was still some distance from her base. The fireworks were over when she approached Pearl Harbor—or so she thought. On the surface, her crew weary from the weeks at sea but keyed up by the realization that war had come, she pushed steadily toward port.

Some planes appeared overhead, but the watch identified them as American and recognition signals were immediately given. It was a comforting sight to see our own fliers dominating the air after the news of what the Japanese had been doing. But not for long.

All submarines looked alike to the planes. They swooped over and let our underwater ship have a rack of bombs. Luckily, this time, the marksmanship was bad. The startled skipper dove in a hurry, his conning tower blue with the language he was using to describe his fellow countrymen overhead. After a considerable time he eased up to periscope depth and looked around. The sky seemed to be clear, so he surfaced and sent a frantic report to the Pearl Harbor submarine base.

Scarcely had he dispatched his message when more American planes appeared, and in spite of the submarine's desperate efforts to identify herself, the fliers made for her and zealously bombed her under again. By now it wasn't funny from any angle. After some time the submarine came up and once more sent out a request that bombers lay off her. But the air forces were too busy seeking revenge for the sneak raid of the Japanese to pass up a chance to bomb a submarine—any submarine. They drove her under again.

Meanwhile the submarine base was begging the Army and Navy Air Force commands to stop trying to sink our own ship. It began to look as though the unfortunate submarine would have to stay below surface for an impossible length of time. Finally, however, the fliers were convinced that she was one of their own, and she was able to get into the harbor.

Such experiences help to account for the fact that all submariners regard planes—all planes—with a doubtful eye. In view of some of their troubles in the early and hectic days of the war, when the bombers sometimes operated with more determination than discrimination, it is not surprising. There is the account, for instance, of an American submarine that was making practice dives off the California coast. She had a couple of destroyers along as an escort, which is the usual practice under such circumstances.

Down the coast came a patrol blimp. The destroyers immediately signaled to the blimp:

"We have a submarine."

"We see her," the reply snapped back from aloft.

And with that the blimp let go her bombs. Luck was with the submarine, and the bombs missed. There is also the instance in which one of our planes bombed a Pearl Harbor submarine shortly after it had started on a reconnaissance patrol toward enemy-held islands. This bombardier was a better shot than some of the others, and scored a near miss that opened up one of the submarine's seams. The ship was able to continue on her way, but wherever she went she blazed an oil trail on the surface of the sea.

These are incidents that happened at the start of the war. Later things were better, and the air forces were convinced that all the submarines in the Pacific didn't belong to the enemy. Our undersea skippers, however, never took anything for granted. When Admiral Kimmel's message about the bombing of Pearl Harbor was sent out, three American submarines were halted outside the harbor. One of them was the USS *Pollock* commanded by Lieutenant Commander Stanley P. Moseley, a stocky, blond officer of the class of 1925 at Annapolis. For two days the *Pollock* hung around, her crew wondering and watchful. Then, on December 9, orders came to proceed to the submarine base.

Moseley and his men didn't stay there long, however. On December 11 they started off on their first wartime patrol, among the first submarines to get underway. In their attempt to run up a good score of Japanese ships, they ran out of torpedoes and returned to base sooner than had been planned. Thus the *Pollock* could claim the distinction of being the first member of our underwater fleet at Pearl Harbor to report the sinking of a Japanese vessel.

The area of the *Pollock*'s first patrol, like those of most of our submarines, was far out—in Japanese waters. She didn't reach it until the last day of the year, but once there she took little time to get into action.

"We went in close to a beach for diving in the morning," Moseley said, "and spent some time looking around. Then we ran into a northeast monsoon, which whipped the waves up ten or eleven feet high. That interfered with our hunting.

We did sight a couple of merchant ships, but couldn't get at them. As a result of our experience, we shifted our position to a better spot the next day. But the current was strong, and we missed the position we were trying for."

Besides the many obvious difficulties and dangers of submarine operations in the enemy's home waters, our ships there were beset by navigation problems—strong currents with which they were unfamiliar, fog, storms, and lack of guiding lights. These factors often made it hard to get into position to fire torpedoes. If it sometimes seems as if a great many torpedoes missed their marks, the circumstances under which they were launched must not be forgotten. As Dr. Samuel Johnson said of a dog's walking on its hind legs, "It is not done well; but you are surprised to find it done at all." In view of the conditions under which our submarines made their attacks, to the layman the fact that they missed frequently should not be so surprising as that they hit the targets at all.

Perhaps the most discouraging thing our submarines were faced with in the early days of the war was defective torpedoes. The experts worked desperately on the problem and largely due to the efforts of Lieutenant Commander J. O. R. Coll, torpedo officer on Admiral Withers' staff, in coordinating the torpedo work, the missiles were made to perform efficiently. It is not hard to understand the feelings of a submarine commander, who, having lined up a target perfectly, finds his torpedoes running erratically, broaching, stopping dead, or even failing to explode when they hit. Bad torpedoes accounted for many of the misses of our submarines on the early patrols.

The *Pollock* went back to her first position on the third day, but "in the right spot" this time.

"We had been there only about an hour when we saw a nice juicy target," Moseley said. "A big freighter. We made an approach and when we had her lined up we fired two torpedoes. The first one hit her just about under the bridge, and immediately after it exploded the freighter went well down by the bow. Water came up under the bridge, and her stern stuck up with the screws showing."

The submariners didn't get much of an opportunity to enjoy their triumph. Japanese planes came across the sky, and as bombs began to fall, the ship dove quickly. "We didn't get another chance to look at the target," Moseley said. "But I'm sure she sank. After that, we decided to shift to another part of our patrol area. On the way over we saw a steamer."

This time heavy weather was working to the advantage of the submarine. She was able to make her approach and line up the target without detection.

"We fired two torpedoes—maybe a third," Moseley said. Then he explained: "We wasted a few torpedoes in the early part of the war. But we hit that Jap ship right under the bridge. We could hear plenty of explosions as we dove for a reload. When we surfaced ten minutes later, she was sinking very rapidly. We watched her go down."

The last sentence recurred again and again in the talk of our submarine commanders. It is almost impossible to describe the air of complete satisfaction with which they always said, "We watched her go down." There is another expression they sometimes used in describing the results of a torpedoing. It brought an equal expression of modest triumph to their faces when they were able to say, "She simply fell apart."

The new area of patrol for Moseley's submarine afforded poor hunting. She prowled around there for two days and although she saw two ships she couldn't get in on them. It was a tight spot for navigation too. The water was too shallow. So Moseley turned his craft and "got out of that place."

"That night it was darker than pitch," the *Pollock*'s captain said. "But one of our lookouts who had good sharp eyes reported a ship on the port bow. A little later he reported that the ship was lying to, so we began our approach on the surface. We were just about ready to let her have a couple of torpedoes when I decided that this time we wouldn't waste one." He grinned a little sheepishly. "You see, we checked our navigation and discovered we were making an excellent approach on a big rock."

By this time the American submarine had only three torpedoes left. It was not until several nights later that she had a chance to fire any of them. The sea was calm; a quarter moon made a nice streak of light, and Moseley's ship managed to get a good-sized freighter, about six thousand tons, directly in the moonbeams. Conditions were ideal from the submarine's point of view. She moved in close.

"We gave the Jap a spread of two torpedoes," Moseley said.

"One of them hit the engine room and there was a tremendous explosion. Smoke and debris flew a hundred feet in the air. The Japs immediately abandoned ship, and they weren't any too soon because she sank in about ten minutes. That left us with only one torpedo. A little later that night we missed a Jap destroyer with it."

Although the *Pollock* had fuel and supplies to stay out longer, there was no point in it with all the torpedoes gone, so Moseley headed her back to Pearl Harbor where he reported her score—three sinkings, all good ones. Her patrol had lasted forty-nine days.

After a rest period for the officers and men and an overhauling and refitting for their ship, the *Pollock*'s commander went to the Flag Office for his orders. Admiral Withers told Moseley, as he was telling so many of our submarine captains, to shove off on the long haul to Japanese home waters.

One diversion for the crew during the long days they pushed on and on to the west was provided by Radioman Wright. All submarine crews have a hunger for news from the world outside. And since the radio provided their only contact, Wright took it upon himself to publish a daily paper which he called Ye Olde Press. This supplemented the magazines which were brought aboard in bales and kept under lock until the submarine was well out to sea before they were distributed.

Putting out a daily newspaper, run off on a typewriter, was a fairly common practice on our submarines, and Sparks usually was the editor and publisher.

At the masthead of his publication, Wright carried this information: "Net Circulation $\frac{1}{10}$ — Net Paid Circulation, None." In addition to pounding out on his typewriter the Navy press news which came in every afternoon, the energetic editor of Ye Olde Press enlivened his columns with "corncob locals"—aimed at various members of the crew.

He had a good nose for news. On one occasion the captain himself had carefully set aside a piece of pie in the refrigerator, but it vanished within a few hours. The very next issue of Ye Olde Press mentioned this act of sabotage and hinted at a pie-eater in the forward torpedo room.

There was another occasion later when Wright apologized because his paper had no news in it. The editor had been too busy shooting torpedoes at the time the Navy press news was coming over the radio.

Upon reaching Japanese waters, Moseley spent a few days moving about in an effort to locate shipping lanes. At last he found what he believed to be an ideal spot, where two lines of traffic appeared to come together.

The Japanese, in turn, seemed to think this might be a good place for a submarine to operate, and Moseley discovered a couple of fishing boats loitering there somewhat like plainclothesmen. He looked them over in the daytime and found they were good-sized sampans, apparently not doing much fishing. The *Pollock*'s skipper disregarded them, however, and that night sighted a freighter of about six thousand tons.

Song and story have described the moon as a friend of lovers; it's also the sweetheart of the submarine men—sometimes. With a nice silvery glow streaming across the water, a target stands out like a cat on a roof peak. Of course, a submarine can make a nice silhouette at times, too. This freighter was sharply outlined but was stepping right along and at a bad angle, so it was necessary to fire hurriedly. Two torpedoes slithered from the submarine's bow. Almost at the same moment the target turned away.

Apparently she had spotted her enemy, and it saved her for the moment. The clumsy sampans tried to join the fight, but the *Pollock* maneuvered around them and took after the merchant ship. For two hours the chase continued. The submarine finally closed up the distance and fell in astern.

The freighter was yawing about five degrees and as she started to yaw to port, her pursuer fired a torpedo into her on the portside.

"She must have been an ammunition ship," Moseley said, "because she blew all to pieces. Before we could turn away, in about a minute, she sank."

The immediate business disposed of, the *Pollock*'s crew manned her deck guns and went for the sampans. It was better than a shooting gallery for the boys on the submarine. They blazed away at one Japanese patrol boat until she caught fire. Then they gave their attention to the other. When the *Pollock* glided away, the first sampan was a great bonfire, and the second was rapidly slipping under the waves.

The submarine resumed her patrol, but soon, with her fuel running low, she started the long-haul home. Honolulu and the Royal Hawaiian Hotel, a couple of weeks of rest and recreation, and Moseley's men were more than ready to shove off. Once more they were ordered to an area close to Japan.

It was while they were in the middle of the Pacific, pushing westward on this patrol, that the captain himself had his biggest scare. He had arranged an emergency signal for him to go on to the bridge. This consisted of ringing his telephone in short blasts until he appeared topside.

"I was sitting in the wardroom playing cards," Moseley said, "when word was passed to me that we had sighted two enemy ships. I couldn't figure why we weren't diving. My heart jumped right into my throat, and I jumped for the bridge. It turned out that the officer of the deck had sent down word that he had sighted the wakes of two enemy ships. That was why he hadn't rung the emergency signal, and why we weren't diving." Moseley snorted.

"Even at that he wasn't right. What he actually had sighted was a couple of tide rips. But he'd given me a shock."

It didn't take the Americans long, after reaching the area of their patrol, to discover that what was spoiling their hunting was too many game wardens—spitkits, sampans, and all sorts of small patrol vessels. At first they were only a nuisance, but gradually they became a real annoyance. So the *Pollock* set about exterminating them. The first one she sighted was a 600-ton combination fishing and patrol vessel.

It was pretty certain that the Japanese vessel had a radio on board just for sending out an alarm if a submarine was sighted. So the *Pollock* submerged and spent six hours sneaking up on the antisubmarine patrol boat. At a range of about one thousand yards she surfaced and opened up in a hurry with machine and deck guns.

The first shell was aimed at the bridge structure. That was where Moseley decided the Japanese probably had their radio. It was a perfect hit and if that's where the radio was it was blown all to pieces before it could say Fujiyama. While still submerged, Moseley, looking through the periscope, had seen men aboard the craft, but after that first shot there wasn't a Japanese in sight. The ship caught fire, began to burn violently. The submarine circled around, but couldn't find any survivors in the water.

As the Americans turned away, the patrol boat was well down at the stern and blazing from end to end. Those aboard her, however, remained below decks, apparently determined to perish in the floating funeral pyre.

For a time after that the Americans ran wild among the Japanese spitkit antisubmarine patrol. Conserving torpedoes and using guns, they went to work on the nuisances. The *Pollock* sank another Japanese fishing-patrol boat about the same size as the one she had left burning to the water's edge. Five more patrol sampans were destroyed in quick succession. In referring to sampans, our submariners are apt to use the term rather loosely to indicate almost any nondescript Japanese boat of relatively small size, rather than a true sampan, although sometimes they mean just that.

But sampan or spitkit, the Moseley submarine disposed of seven before her appetite was satisfied and she continued on her hunt for torpedo targets.

Her next venture was to try to sneak into a Japanese harbor entrance, but an enemy destroyer picked her up.

The *Pollock* made a quick dive to avoid the pattern which the enemy quickly laid down. Unharmed, she managed to slip away. She had been out a long while and time and lack of fuel were beginning to work against her. On a dark night shortly before she headed for home, however, the lookout spotted what appeared to be a large merchant ship on a parallel course. By the time the crew had reached their battle stations, it developed that it was an enemy aircraft carrier traveling at high speed. The submarine let go a spread of four torpedoes. All missed the swiftly moving target. For a little way, the submarine gave chase, but the carrier picked up her skirts and vanished into the night. That was a big one that got away. The men of the *Pollock* celebrated the Fourth of July by arriving back at Pearl Harbor. After almost seven months of whittling at Tokyo's shipping, Moseley was sent back to the United States. He brought a Navy Cross back with him.

14 - 'S' Stands for Stamina

THE LAST SUBMARINE DESIGNATED BY a combined letter and numeral were the S class—the so-called S-boats. We started building them way back in 1916 and before the program was completed fifty-one of these sturdy craft had slid down the ways. Our later types of undersea ships were given names of fish or other aquatic dwellers. At the same time we were laying the keels for the S-boats we also built twenty-seven R-boats, but they were relatively small and useful mainly for coastal patrol.

Originally there were forty-one S-boats 220 feet in length, with a submerged displacement of 1,093 tons and a cruising range of about 5,500 miles. They cost only one-fifth as much as our big modern fleet submarines. The other ten S-boats were only slightly larger but had a cruising range of up to 10,000 miles. All ships of this class normally carried thirty-eight men.

When the war with Japan broke out, the S-boats were regarded as antiques but, over-age though they were, these stout ships and their resourceful and rugged crews gave the Navy one of the happiest surprises of the war. They took an almost unbelievable pounding from enemy depth charges, aerial bombs and gunfire, but with few exceptions survived. They repeatedly caught fire, broke down and plunged to crushing ocean depths. And yet the gallant men who manned these ancient "barrels" somehow managed to keep them going, to scout enemy positions and bases, to sink a large number of Japanese ships.

One squadron of our S-boats, pushed by determined crews, overcame hardships and handicaps to make a 12,000-mile trip from the Panama Canal to Australia. It was accomplished without an escort and with only one stop, at an isolated Pacific island where a base had been hurriedly improvised. Once in the Southwest Pacific, this S-boat squadron won undying fame for the part it played in the blocking of the Japanese drive to invade Australia. Although their limited range placed the S-boats at a disadvantage in a war of vast distances, in one section of our Pacific frontier it didn't make so much difference.

That was in the desolate and fog-drenched Aleutian Islands, which extend some twelve hundred miles west from the tip of the Alaskan peninsula. The farthest of the Aleutians is not even that far from Kuril Strait, which separates Kamchatka Peninsula, belonging to the Soviet Union, from the northernmost of the Kuril Islands, which were part of Japan proper. Based at Dutch Harbor, our S-boats not only patrolled the Aleutians but struck at the enemy in his home waters.

Whatever has been said about the difficulty and hardships of life in a modern submarine goes double for the S-boats. It is tough, and S-boat crews have to be unusually rugged. Sometimes they endured more than would have seemed humanly possible, yet came back to tell about it and start out for more.

The submarine *S-34*, to which A. H. Johnson, signalman first class, was assigned, was one of those which proved beyond question that the S stands for stamina. On her second wartime patrol her captain was Lieutenant Commander T. L. Wogan, who had his orders to go hunting in Japanese waters. The S-boat went first to Attu Island, the westernmost of the Aleutians. This was before the Japanese had gained footholds on Attu, Agattu and Kiska.

From Attu, Wogan headed the *S-34* west, reversing the course which Vitus Bering, the Dane, had sailed two hundred years before as an officer in the Navy of Catherine the Great of Russia. Bering named what are now the Aleutians the Catherine Islands. His own name is kept alive by Bering Island, the Bering Sea, which the Aleutian chain separates from the Pacific, and Bering Strait, where today meets tomorrow at the International Date Line. Wogan's destination was the Kuril Islands, which string out like beads from Hokkaido, the second largest of the main islands of Japan.

After passing through the Kuril chain, the *S-34* headed into the Sea of Okhotsk, which lies between northern Japan and Siberia. At no time is this area pleasant for a submarine, and when Wogan's ship arrived there it was April, cold and foggy. Occasionally she encountered icebergs. With the exception of a lone freighter, that was about all she did encounter.

"We made an approach on that Jap ship and fired one torpedo," Johnson said. "It was a difficult shot and we missed. After that, the captain said he guessed he'd better make Commandos out of us—give us tommy guns and hand grenades and try some shore raids. The whole crew was so eager to get at the Japs, I think he almost meant it."

Wearying of the fog and the icebergs and the lack of Japanese ships, Wogan took the *S-34* back through the Kurils and up into the Bering Sea. Aside from being chased under by a Japanese seaplane, the submarine found no action there and finally headed for home. On the way she received orders to notify the inhabitants of Attu and Kiska that a ship would call to evacuate them; but when she arrived at Kiska, it was so windy and rough no one could get ashore. After lying there all night, waiting vainly for the wind to die down, Wogan's submarine shoved off for Dutch Harbor.

"On our next patrol, the fog played a neat trick on us," Johnson said.

Whenever our submariners talk about their patrols in the Aleutians, they continually mention the thick weather. When it isn't raining in the Aleutian Islands, it's foggy, and when it isn't foggy, it's stormy. To make the area more unpleasant, the sides of the islands, which are of volcanic origin, are steep and ragged. There are few good harbors, but an abundance of reefs, mostly uncharted. Much of the navigation has to be done by guesswork.

Contrary to a common idea, the weather is not extremely cold. The winters are moderate, the temperature averaging around thirty degrees Fahrenheit. This is because of the Japan Current, which sweeps along the island chain; the current also accounts for the heavy rainfall and fog, as warm moisture-laden winds meet the chill air from the arctic or strike the high, cold peaks of the Alaska coastal ranges.

"You know how things look in a fog—all out of shape —and how hard it is to judge size and distances," Johnson continued. "We were moving along cautiously on the surface through a heavy fog when we sighted a ship.

"After maneuvering around we got in a good position and prepared to attack. We were at battle stations and all of us were pretty excited, even if we didn't let on. The captain was at the periscope. My station was in the control room, and I was watching him closely, wondering how soon he was going to pass the word to fire. And then suddenly he gave a laugh and cussed a little." Johnson himself chuckled as he told it.

"After making one of the best approaches a sub ever made, we discovered just in time that we were attacking an island. In another minute we would have sent a torpedo slamming into it. That island certainly looked like a ship through the fog; I got a peek at it through the periscope myself."

Wogan's submarine was in Dutch Harbor when the Japanese bombed that base. Since there was nothing she could do to repel the air invaders, she submerged and lay snug and safe on the bottom of the harbor. When she surfaced, she received orders to proceed to the vicinity of Attu. Word had been received that the Japanese had made landings on that island, the farthest west in the Aleutian chain.

It was raw and windy as the *S-34* pushed westward, with the cold seas breaking over her. The Japanese bombs dropping on Dutch Harbor had erased any doubt as to whether the enemy was in the Aleutians, and the submarine hardly had reached her station when the lookout, peering into the haze, spotted a ship coming toward him.

The submarine made a quick dive and came about. But by the time she was in position to fire her torpedoes, it was too late. Wogan at the periscope was forced to watch a Japanese cruiser, traveling at high speed, fade into the distance.

The Japanese were moving into the Aleutians both by air and by sea. Then the inevitable heavy fog came, a cold, gray blanket that wrapped itself around the submarine.

"It was just the same as being lost," Johnson said. "For two days, we laid a course this way and that. Finally, about six o'clock in the morning of the third day, the captain said we'd go in and see if we couldn't find land.

"The fog had lifted a little, although the visibility was still very low. We moved along slowly on the surface and at last sighted land. This time we didn't mistake it for a ship. We laid a course parallel to the shore and continued on our patrol.

"About an hour later, the quartermaster, who was with the watch, was looking through the glasses. 'Cap'n,' he said, 'I think there's a big rock over there'."

The *S-34*'s quartermaster was not going to be caught stalking a piece of barren land again. "But suddenly he exclaimed: 'No it isn't, Cap'n! It's a ship'."

The submarine dove. Through the periscope Wogan looked the situation over. It was a ship, all right. A Japanese destroyer, a big new one. The crew were at battle stations, ready to torpedo this enticing target, but the fast-moving destroyer slipped out of range and melted into the fog. It quickly developed, however, that Wogan, according to Johnson, had deliberately let the destroyer go. There was something better. Through the mist he had observed it inside a small bay, and he believed it worthy of closer investigation.

The fog was still too thick, so the *S-34* just loafed for a while. Presently the weather began to clear and the submarine, moving closer, brought into her periscope a picture that was enough to make any submarine commander happy.

Inside the small bay lay two ships. One of them was a large tanker, and snuggled up against her, refueling, was a destroyer as large as the one that had just escaped. By now the fog was almost gone, and the entire situation became clear. The destroyer which they had let get away was engaged in patrolling the entrance of the bay and guarding the refueling operations.

"We'll go in and get 'em! Get the big one first," Wogan announced.

The *S-34* started in. The destroyer patrolling back and forth didn't cause her much concern. At periscope depth, she eluded the warship and reached the entrance to the bay. Still at periscope depth, she slipped inside and began to circle slowly around the inlet in her approach on the two-ship target. The Japanese were all at quarters, completely unaware of the *S-34* stealing ever closer, with her torpedo tubes ready and her crew eager.

"I was at my station in the control room," Johnson said, "and I knew we were getting pretty near the target. Then I heard the captain at the periscope say: 'The yellow rats! I could spit in their eye!' I knew then we were dog-gone close." Suddenly a grating sound reverberated sickeningly through the submarine. She trembled from bow to stern.

"I couldn't figure out at first what had happened," Johnson said, "then Lieutenant Sellers, our second officer, told me that we'd run aground!"

The *S-34* had certainly run aground but that was not her only trouble—she had slid onto a ledge and hoisted herself from periscope depth to nineteen feet! A considerable part of her hull was above water, right under the eyes of two shiploads of temporarily panic-stricken Japanese.

Within the American submarine, the momentary consternation swiftly turned to feverish activity. Orders were barked through the ship. In the language of the submarines, "she blew everything"—all tanks that would possibly lighten her, make her buoyant. At the same time, her screws began backing with full power.

The startled Japanese recovered quickly, too. From both the tanker and the destroyer they began firing at the stranded submarine. Deck guns roared out; machine guns added their vicious staccato. And then the second destroyer outside the bay suddenly became aware of what was taking place, and started toward the entrance.

The plucky S-boat and her crew appeared doomed. Wogan was determined that if this was the end it was going to be in a blaze of glory. He passed the order to stand by for battle stations surface. That meant that when all hope of freeing the submarine was gone, the crew would pour up on deck with machine guns and small arms and blast away at the enemy to the last man.

"Things looked pretty bad," Johnson said. "I think some of the boys, including myself, were good and scared, but we weren't showing it—not very much anyway. And we all had our minds made up to get some Japs before they got us."

In reality the scrappy *S-34* was far from knocked out. She began to move. Slowly at first, then faster and faster until she slid off the ledge into deep water. But she was still on the surface and badly crippled, still a perfect target for the shooting of the Japanese. Three of her bow torpedo tubes were jammed, and she had suffered other serious damage, but her hull was intact. Running aground had not opened any of her seams; and the Japanese, caught off balance, were firing wildly. Not a single shot had pierced her so far.

It was impossible for the submarine, in her condition, to maneuver quickly. Fortunately she was headed toward the entrance of the bay, and she started to limp in that direction. The second destroyer came racing in and cut off her escape toward the sea. The S-boat let go a bow torpedo, it was about all the punch she had left.

As the tin fish came boiling toward her, the enemy destroyer tried to dodge it. Almost immediately she found herself in the same fix from which the *S-34* had just escaped—hard aground! The torpedo churned past her and exploded on the beach. It had served a purpose, putting one of the enemy ships out of action for the moment—and it was a precious moment.

The destroyer which had been refueling was now underway. She bore down on the submarine with the obvious intention of ramming her. Wogan dove his ship, but it wasn't a quick dive. She was too battered for that. Heavy and hard to handle as she was, she managed to reach a depth of some sixty or seventy feet before the destroyer roared over, dropping eight depth charges in a bunch; some six thousand pounds of high explosive.

Within the *S-34* the sound of the explosion was thunderous. The concussion rocked her from end to end, and she trembled in every plate. Cork and paint rained down on the sprawling crew, who had been pitched all over the deck. The ship herself was knocked right down to the bottom of the bay.

One hundred sixty-five feet down, she rested in the mud. Three tons of explosive had blasted her at close range. But a checkup revealed that she wasn't leaking a drop. S stands for stamina, all right. Captain Wogan consulted with his officers. It was decided that for the moment no effort would be made to move. The submarine would play dead. Everything on the ship was ordered shut down, except the listening gear.

Absolute silence was imposed, and the captain directed all who were not at battle stations to turn into their bunks. Grimly the men braced themselves to stare death in the face, perhaps for hours. Their situation was desperate; and worst of all, for the time being, there was nothing they could do to help themselves. Nothing to do but sit and wait and think.

"You didn't need any listening device to hear the Jap ships overhead," Johnson said.

"The destroyer and small steam launches were passing back and forth constantly. You could hear them plainly. I sat down at my battle station in the control room. "It was about one o'clock in the afternoon when we went to the bottom," he continued. "I just sat there staring at the clock. It didn't seem to move. And it was cold too, with all the heat shut off. Funny things happened, I remember. We had a machinist's mate first class named Bristol. He had a new flashlight he was very proud of. He was in the control room when the depth charges exploded, and as soon as he picked himself up he ran aft to lay that flashlight down because he didn't want it to get wet!

"Once when I was standing beside the captain, I gave a little sneeze. He told me not to make so much noise.

"Right after we hit bottom, one of the officers turned to me and said, 'Well, this looks like the end. I'm glad I met you.' He didn't seem to be especially afraid or even worried. Just sort of matter-of-fact. I told him I wasn't worrying any, that I thought we'd get out of it.

"Somehow time did pass. But late in the afternoon we got a good scare."

A metallic grating sound ran along the side of the *S-34* from bow to stern. As it broke the tomblike silence of the ship, it sent a chill to the hearts of officers and men. A little later they heard the ominous grating again, and still again. The Japanese were grappling in an effort to locate the submarine on the bottom of the bay.

"We got ready to move if it came again," Johnson said. "What worried us most was that they might hook a line on us and put a buoy on the end of the line. But we got a break. The sound didn't come again. Either the Japs had given up or were grappling in some other part of the bay."

One dragging hour followed another until at last the laggard hands of the clock pointed to eight. Wogan asked to have the time of sunset figured out, and when he was told it would be around ten-thirty, he announced:

"We start out at eleven o'clock!"

That would be ten hours after the *S-34* had plummeted to the bottom. As the time approached for the crippled American submarine to make a last desperate bid to survive, the feeling of relief among the crew was noticeable. At least they were going to do something to help themselves, and to the cooped-up men anything was better than just waiting.

"We finally got underway—slowly," Johnson went on.

"At the start, we had almost no trim at all. One of the screws was damaged and set up a lot of vibration. Then, too, in blowing the ventilating system, we were afraid the bubbles going to the surface would be spotted. But those were things we couldn't help. We just had to trust to luck."

The *S-34* had other troubles. Her after-gyrocompass had been shut down so long it was unreliable. She couldn't even be certain of her directions. Nevertheless, groping along at a depth that varied between 165 and 210 feet, the sturdy American submarine made her way blind across the bay.

But now the *S-34* faced still another major problem: how to locate the narrow entrance that led to the open sea. She accomplished this in a triumph of the resourcefulness and skill of our submariners. The soundman, through his listening gear, discovered that one of the destroyers had taken up a patrol outside the entrance. The destroyer was "pinging"—trying to locate the submarine through his own sound gear. He was working an echo sound device which is used in locating the target for an underwater torpedo shot by a submarine, and for locating a submarine by a surface ship.

In pinging, a supersonic directional beam is swung about. When it is intercepted by the steel of an enemy ship's hull, a pinging noise echoes back. The soundman knows in what direction the vessel lies, since he knows in what direction his beam is turned. But the object of a pinging attempt also can pick up the sound on his gear and knows the enemy is trying to locate him.

Aboard the *S-34* a directional "listening head" caught the ping. Since the submarine's soundman knew in what direction the destroyer was, and knew she was outside the entrance, he therefore knew where the entrance was. And so the Japanese destroyer that was trying to prevent the escape of the submarine actually guided her out of the bay. Sometimes it seems as if there will be no end to a ship's troubles. The *S-34* was in a tight spot.

"When we got outside, that Jap began pinging on us again," Johnson said. "Besides, our ship didn't act right. She was difficult to handle. We played hide-and-seek with the destroyer for three or four hours. Finally she left us alone and began pinging on something else. We headed on out to sea and along about six o'clock in the morning we came up to periscope depth for a look around. "All we could see was fog, so we surfaced. For a while we ran on the surface, and then the captain said we'd make a 'trim dive'."

Already the submarine had escaped what seemed inevitable destruction half a dozen times, and now a simple routine dive almost proved her undoing. She started to submerge. Just as she went under, her crew discovered that the conning-tower hatch was sprung and wouldn't close.

Water cascaded into the conning tower. It was a time for fast action; the men blew everything, and the submarine struggled back to the surface. Except for shipping a lot of water, she was all right but it had been a close call.

Wogan then proceeded on the surface. In a three-word radio message to the base at Dutch Harbor, he summed up some of the most harrowing experiences any submarine ever has gone through:

"Coming home damaged."

At Dutch Harbor, a diver was sent down to examine the ship. He reported that the damage was too extensive to be repaired with the available facilities. The *S-34* was ordered to drydock at Bremerton, Washington.

"On that patrol," Johnson remarked, "I guess everything happened that could have. On the opposite side of the hull from the one the Japs' grapple had scraped, we could see plainly the marks of a giant octopus that had been hanging on to us. We all got liberty in Bremerton, but not a single member of the crew would leave until he'd had a chance to look at the ship in drydock. We wanted to see what the bottom looked like." He shook his head. "The duct keel had been ripped. Half the rudder and the starboard screw were gone. The after part of the superstructure was missing, and the bow had as many wriggles as a hairpin. We had taken a lot, but were all safe and sound."

15 – Submarine Hitchhiker

THE YANKEE SUBMARINE WAS A LONG, long way from home, patrolling off the East China coast. Her base at Pearl Harbor was more than four thousand miles away. It was night, and she was on the surface, charging her batteries and getting some new air inside her hull for the men to breathe when, at dawn, she would slide beneath the waves and continue her relentless hunt for Japan's sea traffic.

One of the two officers on the bridge was the submarine's captain, tall and slender, with dark-brown curly hair and heavy eyebrows, arching over round and intensely blue eyes in a way to give him an expression of constant surprise. That expression was deceptive. Nothing ever seemed to surprise him or upset his balance; he was nerveless and cool-spoken even in the tightest spots. And those are the kinds of spots a submarine in Japanese waters can get into.

The other officer was a blond giant—six feet two inches and two hundred forty pounds of muscle. He was the executive and navigation officer.

Everyone on the bridge, crew and officers, was watching a dark shape off in the darkness. The Americans knew what it was—a Japanese picket boat. The Japanese were looking the submarine over, too, but were fooled by the nonchalant manner in which the undersea boat was moving toward them, and believed it was one of their own craft.

The submarine's executive officer had a machine gun pointed at the picket boat. When they were pretty close, the skipper turned to him and said in a low tone: "Let 'em have it!"

The machine gun chattered angrily. It was good shooting. The first burst hit into the ship's engine and put it out of commission. The men on the picket boat evidently thought they were victims of a terrible mistake. One of them popped out of the cabin waving his arms; he hurriedly offered a recognition signal by illuminating a large rising sun. It made a good bull's-eye for the machine-gunner. His next burst knocked the man into the sea. The bullets continued to rake the enemy craft.

In the midst of the firing, another officer climbed breathlessly through the hatch onto the submarine's bridge. The noise topside had startled him from his bunk, and he was only partially clothed. He was a lieutenant, often referred to as the Wild Irishman, whose favorite expression was "I hate those Japs!" Taking in the situation quickly, he turned to the submarine's commander.

"Cap'n," he pleaded, "let me shoot too."

The skipper hesitated a moment, then grinned a little.

"Well, all right," he said. "Pour it into 'em!"

The Wild Irishman moved onto the "cigarette deck," the space just aft of the bridge where, in the old days, the submariners had to go when they wanted to smoke.

In a few seconds, the staccato bark of a fifty-caliber gun broke forth. When the captain looked up he saw the tracers shooting into the air.

"Doggone it! Hit 'em!" he roared.

"Aye, aye, sir!" came back from the cigarette deck.

But the marksmanship grew worse if anything. Tracers were spitting toward the heavens instead of toward the enemy. What's more, they were wobbling in all directions, like the balls of a Roman candle in the hands of a small boy. The captain stalked aft.

"What the... " he began, then stopped.

The answer was plain—it was a case of over-eagerness. The Wild Irishman had been so anxious to join in the fun that he hadn't bothered to put on his shoes. Now he was standing on his bare feet, with the hot brass shells from the machine gun on them and around them. It was a job for a Hindu firewalker, not a Navy man. The lieutenant was dancing around on the hot shells and at the same time trying to blast the picket boat.

Nevertheless, when the submarine pulled away, the enemy craft was following the same course so many other Japanese ships took—straight down. The captain of the American submarine was Lieutenant Commander Lewis S. Parks, later an aide to Admiral Daubin. His executive officer was Lieutenant Slade Cutter, all-American football player and an intercollegiate boxing champion. The Wild Irishman was Lieutenant Tom McGrath. And the submarine was the USS *Pompano*, named for a fish of the southern Atlantic that is famed for its qualities as food.

"McGrath was the most bloodthirsty man I ever knew," Parks said.

"When we arrived at Pearl Harbor after the raid, I ran into him. His ship had been sunk, and he had no place to go. He was just wandering around homeless, muttering to himself, 'I hate those Japs!' So I arranged to take him along with me."

The *Pompano* had been one of the three submarines coming from the West Coast and had been only a few hours out of Pearl Harbor when the Japanese attacked. She had waited outside the harbor for a while but, being one of our new and most formidable undersea craft, the Submarine Command at the Hawaiian base didn't keep her away from action long. The war was still young when Lew Parks pointed his ship toward the Gilbert and Marshall Islands. The enemy was known to have built powerful sea and air bases on islands in these groups. Indeed, there was a suspicion at that time that they had been used as the springboard for the sneak attack on Pearl Harbor.

Actually, the raiders had come from carriers north of Hawaii. The main purpose of the patrol was reconnaissance, but as always some hunting was permissible. The *Pompano* reconnoitered the area with thoroughness; much of the information she brought back proved useful to our surface forces later when they bombarded the Gilberts and the Marshalls. She also slapped a few torpedoes into a converted luxury liner.

In the course of the reconnaissance, Parks was looking over one of the islands when at dawn, through the periscope, he sighted three ships lying in a harbor. Two were small freighters, but the third was a liner of about seventeen thousand tons, which had been converted into a troop transport. Nothing could have been more welcome to the skipper's eyes.

For three days the *Pompano* hung around the harbor entrance, patiently waiting for her prey to come out. At last, one morning, the Japanese vessel got underway. The submarine maneuvered into a good position, and set the trap. The transport steamed right into it; four torpedoes left the *Pompano*'s tubes to meet her. The first one hit, and at least one other. At the first explosion the big ship began to settle, but the submarine couldn't watch much longer. Patrol boats were boiling out of the harbor and planes came roaring overhead. While the *Pompano* went deep to reload her tubes, her soundman picked up a strange crackling noise—the breaking up of a sinking vessel.

By the time the submarine eased up for a quick look through the periscope, Parks could find no sign of the liner-transport. It was an auspicious beginning, the first act of a smash performance the Americans were about to put on.

The last act took place off the coast of Japan. Lieutenant (j.g.) Ralph Pleatman, USNR, a V-7 officer from the Colorado School of Mines, told about it. The *Pompano* was ordered to patrol off Tokyo Bay, in which area she also would be able to intercept traffic for two other big Japanese seaports, Yokohama and Nagoya. It was the same long, tedious trip that so many of the Pearl Harbor submarines were to make. Nothing to break the sameness except repeated practice dives and drills.

But the crew were putting more zip and zest into them now; the sinking of many Japanese vessels and the bombings and depth-chargings they had dodged time and again had emphasized the value of split-second efficiency. And as the hundreds of miles of turbulent Pacific dropped astern, and day by day the submarine's bow pushed nearer the enemy's homeland, the eagerness of the men mounted. The Americans had been warned that the enemy's anti-submarine screen was not only thick but extended far out to sea. They first encountered it while still hundreds of miles from the shores of Honshu, the largest and most important of Japan's many islands. With little trouble, the submarine maneuvered past the outer ring and drove ahead into the area of big game, the traffic lanes of Japan's bustling seaports.

"When we were about seventy miles from Tokyo," Pleatman said, "we saw a plane and dove. Our hunt had really begun. For several days we patrolled back and forth and made a few unsuccessful attacks. Then we sighted a large freighter of about eight thousand tons.

"We maneuvered to attack, fired one torpedo. It was a hit—right amidships—and immediately the Jap ship took a list to starboard. The captain, however, didn't think she was going down fast enough, so he fired a second one. Just then a destroyer escort, which had been on the other side of the freighter, started for us, down the track of our first torpedo. She ran head on into the second. It must have hit her magazine, because there was a tremendous explosion and she blew all to pieces."

The destroyer was gone in two minutes, and when the *Pompano* closed in to put a second torpedo into the freighter she found the decks were awash, so she left the area without firing again. The news of the disaster had reached the Japanese mainland, however, and planes and ships began to stream out to avenge the freighter and destroyer. Bombs and depth charges whipped up the sea, some of them giving the submarine an uncomfortable shaking.

The *Pompano*'s best lookout was V. Gibson, a torpedoman third class. He also was the submarine's barber. Gibson was a slow-spoken farm boy who had learned to wield a pair of barber's shears in the country by cutting his neighbors' hair. To keep his hand in, he cut all the crew's hair, and after a submarine has been at sea for weeks, the men in her sport some shaggy manes.

When Gibson was on lookout and drawled, "I think I see an airplane," he always saw one. Chief Pharmacist's Mate Joseph Duane, whose quick humor did much to keep the spirits of the submariners up, described Gibson's accuracy. "When anybody hears Gibson say, I think I see …,' Doc Duane declared, "he doesn't wait for more, but dives down the hatch."

During the remainder of her patrol off Tokyo, Parks' submarine had a number of encounters. She made several attacks on Nipponese shipping that were unsuccessful; she evaded heavy bomb and depth-charge attacks with complete success. At last came orders to leave the area and return to her base. Once more, on the surface, the *Pompano* approached the outer ring of the antisubmarine patrol; but this time there was no necessity for sneaking past, and Parks was determined to get one of the patrol craft as a souvenir of his visit to Nippon's shores.

The *Pompano* dove. At a distance of a thousand yards or so, she circled her victim. It was a craft of about eight hundred tons, with depth charges, deck and machine guns and, obviously, radio equipment. But at that, Parks decided, she wasn't worth a ten-thousand-dollar torpedo. The order was passed for battle stations surface. Three hundred feet of fighting American submarine broke through the sea before the eyes of the astonished Japanese, and a moment later her crew were blazing away with deck and machine guns. The first shots were well directed and scored hits. The enemy, however, recovered quickly and began to fire back. The battle was on, with the patrol boat trying to run and the submarine chasing her, the two about fifteen hundred yards apart.

The submarine's first loader slumped to the deck, mortally wounded. A chief gunner's mate, who also was chief of the boat, was wounded in the elbow but stood by his station. As the running fight continued, the Yankee gunners poured some twenty shells at the patrol boat, and many of them hit. Flames broke out and the enemy craft began to sink. The submarine hammered away at her until she slipped beneath the surface. For a few minutes, the victor waited for the depth charges to go off, but after their explosion, which hurled a huge column of water high into the air, she closed in.

Seven survivors were sighted in the water. They were too far from land for any hope of rescue, so a rubber lifeboat was put over and Pleatman and McGrath volunteered to man it. They paddled away from the submarine and approached a couple of Japanese floundering about in the water. But they evidently had been warned about the big bad Americans. They swam away as fast as they could. Pleatman and McGrath tried two more; they were both dead. The last three Japanese visible on the sea also fled from the lifeboat. "We're going to rescue one of those monkeys whether he likes it or not," McGrath muttered. The boat moved close to a frantic Japanese, and McGrath grabbed him. But he refused to be pulled aboard, and fought wildly to get away. McGrath looked at Pleatman.

"There's only one thing to do," he said.

"Let me do it," Pleatman insisted.

He neatly knocked out the recalcitrant Nipponese, and they hauled his limp form aboard.

"He was a chief petty officer in the Japanese Navy," Pleatman said. "Looked just like the caricatures of the Japs—stocky, short-haired, and with a mouthful of buck teeth. We gave him medical attention and food. Was he hungry—he simply gobbled up that food!"

At dawn the morning after the sinking of the patrol boat, the crew of the submarine buried their first loader at sea. He had died the night before, his lungs torn by a bullet. His shipmates sewed his body in clean canvas; it was placed topside with an American flag draped over it and a heavy wrench fastened to the feet. The submarine was stopped upon the rolling swells of the Pacific. As the sun's earliest rays lit up the scene Parks read the Twenty-third Psalm, while all the members of the crew and officers who were not on duty stood with bowed heads. After that, the submarine's captain began to read the Lord's Prayer, and everyone joined in. Then two of the dead gunner's shipmates gently lowered his body over the side, feet first. A little splash, and it vanished into the sea. The submarine turned her bow toward Pearl Harbor.

At the conclusion of the patrol Parks was sent back to the United States, where he joined the staff of Admiral Daubin. He had won a reputation as a cool and daring submarine commander, as well as the Navy Cross and a gold star in lieu of a second Navy Cross. Several of his officers, including Pleatman, also came back to the United States.

The second patrol of the Parks submarine, which preceded the trip to Tokyo, was an unusually successful one. The *Pompano* was ordered to the East China coast. There was a lot of traffic in these waters beyond Japan. The Americans torpedoed and sank a 12,000-ton transport and a 6,000-ton tanker; they machine-gunned and sank a picket boat and a large trawler. The transport was a particularly juicy plum because she was loaded with troops and supplies bound, apparently, for Singapore.

On the way home, the *Pompano* added an interisland steamer to her bag and picked up a hitchhiker.

The submarine was idling along close to some of the small Japanese islands when the window of her periscope disclosed the little steamer. This was not worth a torpedo, so the undersea ship lifted her gray back to the surface and the crew opened up with deck and machine guns. The first three shells slammed into the target, which was fortunate because the deck gun jammed at that point. The steamer came to a dead stop and caught fire. She showed no signs of fight, and Parks closed in until those aboard could hear his voice when he shouted: "Get off! Abandon ship! We're going to sink her!"

There were about forty-five Japanese aboard, Pleatman declared. Forty-four of them were on their knees praying and the other was running wildly around the deck and waving a small white flag. In spite of Parks' warning, which very likely none of them could understand, they made no move to leave their doomed craft. The submariners gave them a couple of bursts of machine-gun fire over their heads. They understood that. They pushed over some life rafts and then one and all jumped over the side, none too soon. Their little steamer was beginning to blaze furiously. This time the Japanese in the water were only a few miles from shore, so the Americans made no effort to pick any of them up. Besides, the area was closely guarded; planes and antisubmarine patrols might appear at any moment.

Suddenly Lieutenant Cutter, who was on the bridge, gave a shout.

"Here he comes! Watch him!"

It was the one lone Japanese who had put more trust in a white flag than in prayers. He was threshing through the water, swimming toward the American submarine as fast as he could. While those topside watched with mingled amazement and amusement, the swimmer reached the submarine and scrambled aboard. They promptly grabbed him.

In very broken English he expressed a desire to go below, and the Yanks accommodated their voluntary prisoner. For the first two or three hours he was so frightened that he couldn't speak or move. He just lay on the deck under the blankets which the Americans spread over him. Little by little he became convinced that he wouldn't be harmed, and he came to life. He was a typical Japanese in appearance, sturdy of frame but shy of meat on it. He was about thirty-five years old and later in his terrible English he informed the Americans that he had a wife and three children at Choysi Ko, a suburb of Tokyo. Although he didn't know it, he had swum right into the distinction of being the first Japanese prisoner taken by a submarine.

The crew weren't certain what to feed him at first, but having learned in school that rice and tea were staples of the Japanese diet, they offered him these. Togo, as the crew immediately named him, showed little enthusiasm, but when he saw the submariners eating steak and potatoes, pie and coffee, his eyes brightened. He pointed eagerly to the American food and then to his open mouth.

They changed his menu, and Togo gained twenty pounds on the way to Pearl Harbor, some of which undoubtedly was due to the layers of sugar and ketchup he put on everything he ate.

Togo would have been a success in any submarine and he made a smash hit with Parks' crew. In the first place, he quickly indicated that he wanted to help, so they made him a messboy for the crew and he outworked all the others. Soon he was No. 1 messboy aboard. He also was a one-man show, entertaining his captors with card tricks and one-handed knot tying.

Togo enjoyed the submariners and the submariners enjoyed Togo. In fact, the crew wanted to take him out on the next patrol, he was such an excellent messboy, and when this was impossible, they gave him clothes, cartons of cigarettes, toilet articles and candy bars before he departed for internment. They all wanted to know where he was going to be confined so they could go out and visit him.

At only one point on the voyage home did Togo's good humor and spirits fail him. Upon learning that his destination was Honolulu, he was terribly upset. When he had first seen the American submarine he had got the idea that she would be going to San Francisco. Togo had relatives there. He thought he was thumbing a ride to the Golden Gate.

16 – "Govern Yourself Accordingly."

THE TROPICAL NIGHT WAS BRILLIANT with stars, and the warm air brought the fragrance of lush growths from the interior of the island. In the little harbor an American submarine lay at anchor. It was a night for sleep, a night for pleasant dreaming. The submarine's captain had taken full advantage of it. He had placed a cot topside and stretched out beneath the sky. If he dreamed, it probably was of that happy day, still a year distant, when he would complete his duty on the Asiatic Station.

Above, the scene was one of calm and peace; below, in the radio room, Sparks was hunched over his dials. His expression was tense, serious. He beckoned to a shipmate, showed him a message he had taken down. The sailor headed topside. Scrambling up the ladder with the agility of a monkey, he burst onto the deck and ran to the captain's cot. He gave the red-haired skipper a little shake and gasped:

"Cap'n! Cap'n, we got to get out of here! The Japs have done it!"

The sailor's excited words exploded in Red Coe's consciousness. He hit the deck, all six feet two of him. Seconds later, he was reading the dispatch which electrified our Asiatic naval forces into action. "Japan has started hostilities Govern yourself accordingly."

The submarine, one of our S-boats, was lying in the little harbor at Masbate town on the island of that name, almost in the middle of the Philippines. She was one of a number of undersea craft which Admiral Hart had stationed at strategic spots for this very contingency.

"That message meant just one thing to me—get out and get in the middle of the strait," said Red Coe—on the records, Lieutenant Commander J. W. Coe, native of Richmond, Indiana, and class of 1930 at the Naval Academy. Within a few minutes, the *S-39* was underway. On the surface, she moved swiftly out of the harbor and headed for San Bernardino Strait, which opens into the Pacific Ocean on the eastern side of the islands. It was still night. Below decks, the excited crew were grimly readying and checking the submarine's instruments of destruction.

Dawn came upon the *S-39* as she was entering the western end of the strait and as it grew light she submerged. About six o'clock, Coe sighted a merchant ship standing out of the strait.

To the eager submariners, this seemed almost too good to be true. They began an approach on the target and soon had maneuvered into a good firing position. The tubes were ready. Throughout the ship, the men waited for the word from the skipper that would send the torpedoes on their way; but Coe was studying the freighter through the periscope. She bore no mark of identification, flew no flag. Instead of making a torpedo attack, he ordered battle stations surface, and the *S-39* shoved up through the waters of the strait into the daylight.

"We tried to signal him," Coe said, "but could get no answer. Finally we fired a round of four-inch across his bow. When the deck gun went off, the boys below knew the war was on. It also stopped the merchantman, and we went alongside. Just as I suspected, the ship was a Filipino. Those on board didn't know war had broken out. When we told them, they were wall-eyed. We sent them back to Manila."

The *S-39* continued to scour the area. Coe's relatively small and aged submarine was the lone representative of the vaunted naval might of the United States in those waters. But less than three years later—October 24 and 25, 1944—the Second Battle of the Philippines was to be fought in this general area. Then we were to hurl our powerful Seventh and Third Fleets against the cream and bulk of Japan's navy. We were to smash the Japanese with ships, planes and submarines. We were to sink twenty-four of the sixty ships the enemy sent into the battle, including two battleships, four carriers and twelve cruisers.

Of the rest, only two enemy craft would escape damage. We would lose two escort carriers, two destroyers and a destroyer escort.

For destruction of the enemy's sea power the Second Battle of the Philippines was our greatest victory of the Pacific war. The Japanese never recovered from the blow. It was a different story, however, the second week of December 1941, when Coe received information that enemy ships were coming into Legaspi, a large and important harbor on Luzon, a few miles north of San Bernardino Strait.

The Americans headed up there. Early in the morning of December 13, before daylight, they were off the mouth of Legaspi Bay when they sighted what they took to be a small patrol vessel circling. The *S-39* started in for her. As the Yank submarine closed in, the patrol craft began to look like a submarine on the surface. It was still an hour before dawn.

The Americans submerged in order to sneak up on their target. It was too dark to see through the periscope, but they could hear the other craft on the sound gear. Just as it was growing light enough to make out the enemy, he submerged. The Americans still could hear the Japanese submarine, and there was no doubt the Japanese could hear them.

"About then, we picked up a beautiful Jap merchant ship coming in toward the harbor," Coe said, with a broad smile.

Leaving the enemy submarine, the *S-39* started an approach on the new target and by the time it came within range had worked into a pretty good firing position. Three torpedoes leaped from the bow and toward the incoming freighter. At the periscope, Red Coe watched intently.

"I was hypnotized by the sight of the big Jap flag she was flying," he said. "I wanted to see what happened. It was a mistake. When I swung the periscope around, there were four Jap destroyers coming out of the harbor, evidently to keep a rendezvous with the incoming ship."

The water was smooth, and the torpedo tracks were as plain as a cow path in a meadow. At about the time Coe discovered the destroyers, one of the torpedoes hit the merchantman with a terrific explosion. The S-39's skipper took a look and saw she was on fire amidships and well heeled over. Even while he watched, she started going down. But by this time the nearest destroyer had located the submarine through the torpedo tracks and was firing at the periscope with a deck gun.

Coe's undersea ship dived deep. Inside her the men could hear the Japanese warships milling around overhead, and every second they expected the depth charges to start exploding. All the machinery on the submarine was shut down, including the air conditioning. Soon there were little pools of sweat around each man's feet. But still no depth charges. The Americans were mystified, and they didn't like the waiting.

"I wish they'd start and get it over with," Lieutenant Larry Bernard, the ship's second officer, muttered.

The Japanese, however, didn't start; instead, sound reported in a little while that the destroyers had faded out. The submarine came up and poked her periscope through the millpond surface of the sea. Instantly the order rang out to go deep. A quick look had shown Coe that they were in the middle of a square formed by the four destroyers which were drifting on the surface with their engines shut down. They had been trying to trap the American submarine and had almost succeeded.

Again the S-39 shut down everything, but still no depth charges came from the destroyers. After an hour or so, with the aid of a strong current, the submarine was carried into the strait and got clear. The Japanese tried one other trick, but it also failed to work. One of the S-boat's officers reported a floating mine, and a little later another. The enemy had thrown them overboard on the chance that the submarine would hit them when she surfaced.

The Americans finally decided that the Japanese submarine had saved them from a depth-charge attack. The destroyers knew she was somewhere nearby under the surface and were afraid to dump their ashcans lest they blast their own submarine.

That night, as the S-39 ran on the surface and charged her batteries, some of the members of the crew who were not on duty listened to the radio. They tuned in Radio Tokyo and gleefully heard the Japanese announcer tell of an engagement with a strong American force off Legaspi.

Unfortunately Japan had lost a merchant ship, the announcer said, but this was more than made up for by the sinking of an American submarine.

The S-39 crew didn't feel sunk at all; they were in high spirits.

After a few more days Coe took his ship back into Manila just in time to see the Japanese bomb the area.

"There was no rest for the weary," the captain said. "For a week, we had to work all night and flop on the bottom of the bay during the daytime."

When the *S-39* finally set out again, she was ordered to patrol down through the Philippine Islands and on to Java. The voyage was uneventful until she reached the Sulu Sea, which separates the Philippines and Borneo. There one day, as she pushed southward, the officer at the periscope was taken aback momentarily to see another periscope in his eyepiece. The S-boat swung quickly, took a potshot at the enemy submarine, but nothing happened. The soundman, however, reported that the Japanese also had sent a torpedo in their direction. And that was that—neither underwater fighter saw or heard anything more of the other.

Coe's ship arrived in Surabaya under circumstances similar to those of her arrival in Manila. She was just in time for the start of the daily bombing, and again she flopped on bottom while the sun was up. By night, the Dutchmen at the naval base, working heroically, overhauled their ally's undersea ship.

On her third patrol the *S-39* headed for Singapore. Finding no enemy shipping in that part of the South China Sea, she started south again. Things began to look up. What appeared to be a Japanese convoy came over the horizon. As the blurs took shape, they resolved themselves into four destroyers, three cruisers and an aircraft carrier. Word of the enemy line-up spread quickly through the submarine, and presently one of the men approached the skipper.

"Cap'n," he said, "there must be some mistake. Those seven ships must all be destroyers. We've been checking off the radio reports of sinkings, and the Japs haven't any cruisers left."

This was an encouraging assumption, but the captain had no chance to check on it. The ships zigged off and were too far away for the S-boat to get a shot at them. It was a blow to the Americans to watch this rich assortment of targets fade into the distance without ever having come within range, but scarcely an hour later a large naval tanker came wallowing along to cheer them up. This time they not only got within range, but in a good firing position.

Four torpedoes were launched in the tanker's direction. With gratifying regularity came the sound of three explosions, one after another. But there was no fourth. One of the tin fish had kept right on going. Three for four is nice hitting in any league, but Coe's men aimed at perfection.

"The torpedoman rushed back to the control room," the captain said, "and he was almost frantic. He wanted to know what I thought had happened to our other torpedo, as if he couldn't believe that it had missed."

The tanker was mortally wounded, with three gaping holes in her hull, but the Japanese made no move to abandon her. Instead, they put on all their pumps and made strenuous efforts to save her. Meanwhile the *S-39* stood off and watched their futile antics. Every member of the crew was given a chance to come to the periscope and take a peek at their prize. It was a prize—fourteen thousand tons of ship. After fifty minutes, the tanker slid into her watery grave.

The submarine got out of the way. Soon the soundman reported the screws of destroyers and the Americans knew help had arrived in time to pick up survivors. The warships passed overhead, unaware that the cause of all their grief was hiding so near. No depth charges were dropped, and soon the sound of the screws faded out. A little later, however, there were a couple of explosions fairly close, which were identified as aerial bombs. At about the same time the diving officer, Lieutenant Guy Gugliotta, reported to Coe:

"Cap'n, this is either the best trim we've ever had, or we're sittin' on bottom."

No matter what he did, Gugliotta said, nothing happened. It quickly developed that the submarine indeed was sitting on bottom in the shallow water of the Java Sea. More than that, her screws had been churning up the mud, sending a murky column to the surface like an Indian smoke signal. This had enabled a plane to spot her and drop the bombs.

The submarine went up a little and got clear. Then she proceeded on her way toward Australia. At Fremantle, Coe was relieved of his command of the *S-39*. He left her not without considerable regret and took over the command of another and larger undersea fighter. In his new submarine—the USS *Skipjack*—Red Coe set forth again for the South China Sea.

The *Skipjack* was a large modern fleet submarine, quite different from the old *S-39*. Her area of patrol was off Camranh Bay, and when Coe arrived there, he bumped into good luck almost at once. A ship was sighted coming down.

It was about an hour before dawn. On the surface, the submarine made an end run around the target, as Coe described it, until she had reached a point about seven miles ahead, and there she dove. With her tubes ready, she waited. Just as the first streaks of dawn broke in the east, the freighter began to come within range. Coe looked her over carefully: about six thousand tons and heavily loaded.

Her decks were piled high with crates and boxes. As the unsuspecting freighter pounded along at about ten knots, the *Skipjack* gave her a spread of three torpedoes. One of them blew into her hull just under the bridge, tearing her wide open. Coe turned the periscope over to his second officer, Lieutenant Giff Clementson, so he could verify the sinking. Clementson surveyed the debris and wreckage that was tumbling into the sea; boxes and crates were bobbing all around the stricken freighter.

"It looks like they're dumping garbage," Clementson said.

Coe took another look. The Japanese ship was going down bow first, with her screw out of the water. The captain summoned the chief torpedoman to look at the results of his work. By this time the Japanese were jumping off the doomed craft and swimming. As he watched, a broad smile of satisfaction covered the chief's face—he had seen the enemy take her death plunge and disappear beneath the waves, all in less than two minutes. Once more the captain took over the periscope.

Hundreds of boxes were floating about where the ship had been, and about twenty-five of them had Japanese, in their underwear, perched on top. It was five o'clock in the morning, and the sinking had taken place close to a lighthouse, so the submarine pulled clear.

For the next few days the *Skipjack*'s patrol was routine—the tedious and nerve-straining task of hunting the enemy without any action to relieve the tension. Then she picked up a small convoy, three cargo ships and a destroyer, and the world began to look brighter. The biggest of the freighters was about ten thousand tons and looked as if she had a deck load of planes. This one, obviously, was made to order for the submarine.

The *Skipjack* slipped in from the side away from the destroyer escort and fired two torpedoes at the bulky target.

Both of them smacked the freighter right in the middle. She broke in two like a huge letter V and started down, while those aboard her fought desperately to launch their lifeboats. Again Coe called Clementson to the periscope to verify the sinking.

Meanwhile, confusion and panic had seized the other two cargo ships. Even the destroyer was running around like a puppy chasing its tail. But the officers and crew of the submarine were working smoothly and coolly. They swung their ship around, and more torpedoes churned toward the remaining freighters and the destroyer, this time from the submarine's stern tubes. She scored another hit in the stern of one of the cargo vessels but the destroyer avoided the tin fish and started to close in on the submarine. As he started deeper, Coe took a final look at his newest victim. The ship was going down at the stern.

For a while the enemy destroyer gave the submarine a working over with depth charges but the *Skipjack* finally slipped clear when the warship went back to pick up survivors from the two torpedoed merchantmen.

Evidence that the Nipponese willfully scorned the articles of the Geneva Convention and the accepted rules for the conduct of war is overwhelming. The land forces time and again caught the Japanese turning the symbols of mercy, which to civilized nations spell immunity from attack, to their own treacherous purposes. Our submarine commanders frequently ran into more or less obvious trickery. Red Coe had this experience on this first patrol in his new command.

"It was an unusual happening," he said. "Just before dark one day, we saw two cargo ships. They evidently spotted us too because they started zigzagging. As one of them zigged away, I noticed a red cross painted on the bridge. There were no other markings. But there were guns fore and aft."

Red Cross markings and guns don't go together on a ship: they're a flat contradiction. Coe, however, elected to disregard the guns and give to the red cross painted on the bridge the benefit of the doubt. He turned his attention to the second ship and began an approach. It was still light enough to see through the periscope, and as the submarine closed in, the captain discovered that the second craft also had a red cross painted on her bridge. She also had guns mounted fore and aft. This time the Yankee skipper reversed himself and chose to be guided by the guns. He fired two torpedoes. Just as they left the tubes, he was alarmed to see two nurses standing below the bridge. There was something wrong about the whole setup, but Coe nevertheless felt badly while the torpedoes were streaking through the water.

They both missed, and then he felt better—the only time he ever welcomed a miss. Not until the *Skipjack* was ready to head back for her base did she run into any more action. Just before leaving the South China Sea, she sighted a pair of ships. A long end run around them put the submarine in position for a submerged attack. The targets were two transports, a small one ahead of a larger one. In order not to disclose her position, the *Skipjack* let the first go by. She fired two torpedoes at the second and scored a hit under the bridge.

The explosion was violent. It opened up the side of the ship and split the tops of her fuel tanks. The submariners could see the oil streaming down her side. Both enemy ships began firing their deck guns at the periscope; on the stricken craft, the crew manned the lifeboats. As the big transport went down, the smaller ship started back to pick up survivors, her guns blazing at the periscope. The submarine was ready for her and let go with a couple of torpedoes, but the Japanese ship was moving fast and going through radical maneuvers. Both missed.

Word came to Coe from below that his men could hear bullets hitting the deck, so the submarine ducked. When she came up again, within five minutes, for another shot at the enemy, the Japanese ship had picked up the survivors and was racing toward the horizon.

On his return from this patrol, Red Coe was awarded the Navy Cross. Four of his men were advanced in rating, and the chief of the boat, Chief Torpedoman Richardson, who had previously been recommended for promotion, was advanced to warrant officer. His work had been so outstanding on this patrol that Coe recommended him for a commission. When he next came back from patrol, Richardson was made an ensign. Amboina Bay was the *Skipjack*'s next destination. This was a lively area in the East Indies, but Coe and his men stayed on the station between two "hot" periods and the results failed to measure up to their hopes. The Japanese in this area were using a great many sailboats, which were apparently engaged in fishing, but our submarine commanders noticed that these spitkits were always on hand when a vessel entered or left the harbor, probably to act as lookouts or as an antisubmarine patrol.

The Americans nevertheless managed to make some attacks on the enemy. A few miles from the entrance to the bay, they sighted a small merchant ship and made an approach. Two torpedoes were fired and both missed, although conditions seemed excellent. Two other submarine commanders, according to Coe, had an identical experience in the same area, and they concluded that the Japanese were using ships of shallow draft camouflaged to appear as much larger vessels.

The *Skipjack*, however, took revenge for this trick before she left the area. She sighted a 14,000-ton naval tanker, a sister ship of the one Coe had sunk with the *S-39*. This time he also got in a good hit, but the tanker's escorts drove the submarine under before he could see the enemy vessel sink, so he claimed credit only for damaging her.

The cook on the *Skipjack* was an unusually good one, but he pretended that the enormous appetites of the submariners griped him. While off Amboina, the Japanese antisubmarine patrol got after Coe's ship and started a heavy ash-canning just before the crew normally would have eaten supper. Pots and pans were bounced around the galley and the cook had his hands full. When the submarine finally pulled clear, the crew kidded him for not having a hot supper prepared for them at the usual time.

The cook threw up his hands. "What are you gonna do with a bunch like this? For a while, I didn't think I'd ever have to cook another meal for 'em. Now all they can think of is filling their stomachs."

Japanese-held islands in the Western Pacific were the area of Red Coe's last patrol in the war zone before he was sent back to new construction in the United States.

The *Skipjack* reconnoitered enemy positions and, although there was only one Japanese ship in her bag at the finish of the patrol, it was one that brought immense satisfaction to the submariners.

Hunting was poor as the submarine made her way northward through the East Indies, and it was a relief when, on emerging into the Pacific, she sighted a large enemy vessel. The sharp eyes of M. M. Holman, a machinist's mate second class, deserve the credit for this one. They earned their owner an advance in rating to first class. Holman was on lookout when he called attention, at the close of the day, to a peculiar wisp of cloud on the horizon. No one else could see it at first and small wonder—it was twenty-three miles away. At that, it was only a puff of smoke, not a cloud. But soon it developed into the hazy outline of the enemy ship.

During the night the *Skipjack* chased the target for one hundred twenty miles in order to get into position for an attack. As the ship loomed up in the window of the periscope at daylight, Coe could make out her deck cargo plainly—airplanes! And she was standing in for Rabaul, where the Nipponese had established a large and important base.

Our air forces never had to bother to shoot down those planes. They're lying somewhere on the bottom of the ocean, along with the ship that was carrying them. The submarine's torpedoes blew her wide open. The *Skipjack* pointed her bow toward Pearl Harbor. War had come to the Pacific and Red Coe, in two different ships with two different crews, had indeed governed himself accordingly.

Like the *Sea Raven*, the *Skipjack* ended her career as a guinea-pig boat in the Bikini atom bomb tests.

17 – Bell-Bottom Trousers

Singin'
Bell-bottom trousers
And coats of Navy blue
He'll learn to climb the riggin'
Like his daddy used to do!

IT'S SUNG THROUGHOUT THE NAVY, but it's a special favorite with the submariners, this "Bell-Bottomed Trousers." It's an old English song of obscure origin, which our Navy adopted. It has also been adapted. During the latter part of the war one of our brighter songwriters modernized the lyric, although he left the tune fairly intact, and "Bell-Bottom Trousers" became one of the biggest popular song hits of 1945.

Submariners like to sing; and when they returned from long patrols and got together for relaxation, their parties rang with robust ballads. Then admirals brought out ukuleles and four-stripers played chords on the piano for the singers. Our submarine officers and crews both fought hard and played hard.

In the submarines they have their own bards too, and almost every division has its song or songs, usually to some familiar tune. There's one they sing in the service, written by some unidentified lyricist, which lets the rest of the Navy know how the men in the submarine fleet feel about their job.

The battleships are mighty,
The backbone of the fleet;
Aircraft and destroyers
Are mighty hard to beat;
The armored cruiser squadron
Is known on land and sea,
But any greasy submarine
Is home, sweet home, to me.

The Navy has not only its own songs, but also, of course, its own legends. A number of these are built around Captain Joe Fife, one of the most rugged characters ever to serve in the United States Navy. Captain Joe lived in the days of wooden ships and iron men, but he is still a favorite with submariners, and his quick wit and vigorous personality would have been well suited to submarine life today. The stories about the doughty captain are countless. They're told and retold in the Navy, and sooner or later every young officer and many of the enlisted men hear most of them.

Captain Joe is the Paul Bunyan of the wardrooms. On one occasion he was in command of four frigates that were faced with the problem of negotiating the Strait of Magellan against a heavy tide and a strong headwind. The squadron included some steam gunboats, and these were hooked onto the four sailing vessels to tow them through. But even that was difficult, and after a bit the skipper of the gunboat that was towing Captain Joe's flagship sent back the message: "Unless the wind and the tide abate, I cannot tow you through the strait." The gunboat's captain had not realized that he had sent his message in rhyme, but Captain Joe noticed it and immediately sent back the answer: "As long as you have wood or coal, haul away, doggone your soul!"

It may be a surprise to learn that in the days of Captain Joe Fife the feminine influence was even stronger in the Navy than it is today, and decidedly on a more personal basis. It is true, nevertheless—some of the officers were allowed to take their wives along with them on their wooden warships in peacetime. The captain and executive officer, at least, were very likely to have their wives on board.

The Navy, however, finally decided that this arrangement should be modified. The Bureau of Navigation issued orders that on the Asiatic Station no wives were to be allowed aboard the ships. But once when Captain Joe pulled into Yokohama, the first person to come aboard was Mrs. Fife. What's more, she refused to get off; she had journeyed all the way from the United States on a passenger ship to join her husband, and she meant to stay.

To Captain Joe, true Navy man that he was, orders were orders. He promptly reported his wife to the chief of the Bureau of Navigation for disobedience to orders. Furthermore, he charged the chief of the bureau with being partly to blame, because he had supplied her with the money to get to Yokohama. The chief was Mrs. Fife's father. Perhaps the best of all the Captain Joe yarns has its setting at Gibraltar, where the Captain's flagship was lying at anchor on the occasion of Queen Victoria's birthday.

This called for a salute by the American ship in honor of her Majesty. Twenty-one guns were made ready for firing, and, as was the custom, a twenty-second gun also was loaded, to be fired in case any of the twenty-one failed to go off. That's what happened. One of them hung fire, and so the stand-by gun was promptly touched off. Then, to the embarrassment of the Yankee gunners, the supposedly dead cannon suddenly came to life and went off. The result was a salute of twenty-two guns.

This was a terrible situation. It contained all the elements of a diplomatic crisis. It was dynamite—but Captain Joe Fife was equal to it. As the Americans expected, a small boat immediately put off from the British Admiral's flagship, and soon a flag lieutenant was piped over the side and ceremoniously escorted to Captain Joe's quarters. What in the name of naval tradition, asked the lieutenant, was the idea of twenty-two guns? Or didn't the American captain know that twenty-one was the proper number?

"Go back to your admiral," boomed the Yankee skipper, "and tell him that twenty-one guns were for her Majesty the Queen, and one gun was for Joe Fife, by golly!"

The Navy also has innumerable contemporary tales, both tall and true, and many of the best come from the Submarine Service. One of them, a story about a colored messboy and his remarks during his first depth-charge attack began to make the rounds in the early days of the war. It was retold so often that four versions were circulating, but since the incident occurred on Fenno's submarine and the messboy's words were spoken to him, his account is the correct one and probably the best one.

Fenno's submarine was undergoing a heavy depths charging from destroyers off the coast of Japan. Everyone was at his battle station. The charges were exploding all around, shaking the ship and giving the crew the jitters. Fenno made an inspection to be sure that everything was all right. Finally he came to the linen locker, where the colored messboy had his battle station. The lad was leaning against the side of the locker, headphones clamped tightly to his ears, his eyes rolling. When he saw the skipper, he managed a weak grin.

"Cap'n," he said, "them Japs sure are mad at us!"

How long does it take to get down the hatch in a quick dive? By actual test with a stopwatch aboard Mike Fenno's modern submarine at the Portsmouth navy yard, Robert Ray Morford, radioman third class, went from the lookout platform to the bridge, through the hatch and down the ladder to the deck of the conning tower in two and four-fifths seconds.

"I can do better when a destroyer is after us," he said modestly.

The worst experience Electrician's Mate Robert E. L. Williams ever had was in the *S-33*, skippered by Lieutenant Commander David C. White. Williams, an undersea veteran, got into the submarines because of a trick he played while a seaman on the old *Oregon* when she was a submarine tender.

"I had a knot trick—put a bowline on a bight and then ran a bowline through it," Williams said. "It was very difficult to do, and I had a bosun who couldn't untie it. I could untie it behind my back. That made him sore, and the first chance he got he shot me to the subs."

Williams's most harrowing experience occurred off the coast of Japan when White's submarine was driven down by depth charges at 8:33 one night and stayed under until 9:30 the next night—twenty-five hours in an antique ship!

"We were at battle stations all that time," Williams said. "We slept at our stations and they brought our food to us. There was no heat and it got good and cold. The can was very low. Finally the captain said, 'We come up now—or we don't come up.' We came up, but we just barely made it. I was really in love with my submarine from the start, but for a while there I almost wished I was back on the old Oregon."

Just sinking enemy ships isn't enough for our submariners; they take advantage of their function as attackers and bet and organize pools on these sinkings.

John Delmont Rogers, electrician's mate second class, recalls an optimistic bluejacket on his ship who made bets each day that they would sink an enemy vessel. He kept doubling up, and before long he was way in a hole. But he talked to the captain: "Cap'n, think we'll get one today? Let me take her, Cap'n, I'll get one."

Apparently he knew what he was talking about, because he wound up about fifty dollars ahead, according to Rogers. Some of the reports radioed in by our submarine commanders far at sea are gems of humor, and others compress into a few brief words a volume of drama. There was, perhaps, a hint of annoyance in the one Lieutenant Commander Parks once sent:

"For the third time, this vessel has acted as target for enemy depth-charging."

Do they ever have pets on a submarine? We-e-ll, no, not officially. In the old days, they used to carry canaries and white mice in order to learn from the action of these creatures when the air was getting bad. Nowadays, delicate instruments supply this information. Newspaper stories of the exploits of British Submarines occasionally mentioned the annoyance caused by the large numbers of rats aboard.

Do we have rats on our submarines? As Admiral Withers put it, "A rat would starve to death on one of our subs."

The insignia of the Submarine Service is a pair of dolphins holding in their mouths the bow planes of an onrushing submarine. Before the war, to qualify as a submarine officer and wear the dolphins a candidate had to spend two years on duty in surface ships before he could be transferred, six months at the Submarine School, and a year of active duty in submarines. Then he could take the examination given by the board. If he passed, he could be recommended for qualification. During the war a submarine commander could recommend that any of his officers be certified as qualified submarine officers.

Civilian Recruitment Poster

18 – Breaking the Jinx

WHEN LIEUTENANT COMMANDER E. E. ("STEAM") Marshall arrived at Pearl Harbor in June 1942, to take over one of our submarines as relief commander, he discovered he was to skipper a hard-luck ship. His command was the USS *Cuttlefish*.

Manned by an eager crew, the *Cuttlefish* had patrolled steadily since the start of the war, but had sunk no enemy vessels. Wherever she had gone, the hunting had been poor. A cuttlefish is a small and ugly denizen of the deep with numerous arms, a sort of little cousin to the octopus, and relatively slow-moving. The latter was one of the handicaps of the submarine named for it. Marshall's ship was the first of the large fleet submarines, but she was slow because she was equipped with only two diesel engines, instead of the four installed in later ships of her class.

The submarine's new captain was determined to break the jinx. When he received his orders for the patrol, however, it looked as if fate was still conspiring against his craft. Her destination was a "gambler's area," off the coast of Japan. On the basis of the best information available, there would be little or no merchant shipping there and only a faint possibility that the submarine would encounter naval vessels. It wasn't very encouraging. But as Marshall's new command sailed toward the setting sun, the omens became more favorable. She had entered enemy waters and was running submerged in the daytime when the soundman picked up a submarine.

The American submarine started after the enemy fast, and was getting into an attack position when the Japanese submarine dove. Then began a deadly game of blindman's buff. Both ships were below periscope depth and for an hour they milled around, chasing each other, each trying to get a sound bearing on the other for a literal shot in the dark. After a while, the Japanese craft went deep, and the Americans lost it. They had held their fire; sound reported, however, two torpedoes shot by the Nipponese submarine, both wide of the mark.

The skirmish was inconclusive, yet it was a tonic for the officers and crew. Once more the *Cuttlefish* pushed on toward the shores of Japan. For the first ten days in her area, she patrolled close to the coast, but her only contact with the enemy consisted of being driven under a few times by planes, and her only battle was with the strange ocean currents.

On one occasion, while the submarine was running on the surface, something needed fixing on the bridge, and the electrician was summoned topside. He was halfway up the hatch when a plane appeared and the diving alarm was sounded. The unlucky electrician was caught in the cascade of men coming below. They knocked him backwards into the conning tower, and he landed with a crash on the deck.

His dignity and his head both suffered bumps. He was the ship's only casualty. The men began to tire and showed signs of strain, so Marshall pulled out to sea in order to give them rest and relaxation, as well as to air out the boat and charge the batteries. Cruising on the surface, the submarine sighted a small trawler one afternoon. The spitkit wasn't worth a torpedo, and the captain decided to sink her with gunfire.

As soon as a description of their target was passed to the men below, the crew became convinced for some reason that it was a "Q-boat." This was the name applied to the decoy ships which the British used in World War I. They were camouflaged as fishing craft or other apparently harmless vessels, but were heavily armed and fully equipped with depth charges. These mystery ships have always appealed to the public's imagination and in a way they appealed even to the crew of the *Cuttlefish*.

Some of Marshall's men liked to draw. Sketches were tacked up almost daily on the bulletin board; they caricatured most of the exciting or humorous happenings on board. When the submarine had engine trouble, it inspired a picture of the chief machinist's mate catching parts in a basket. The officer of the deck, a confirmed pipe smoker, was portrayed on watch with a cloud of smoke enveloping him, the lookout excitedly reporting a steamer on the horizon.

When the artists heard of the impending attack on the spitkit, they soon had a large drawing posted. It showed a cross section of the target, its mast a periscope, depth charges all through the boat and the sound equipment represented by the three-ball sign of a pawnbroker. On the bow sat a Japanese with a fishing line. Beneath the baited hook, was the American submarine coming up with a wide-open mouth. This masterpiece bore the caption: "Sucker bait."

Whether this diagnosis was correct they never found out. Just as the submarine was about to make a battle surface, one of the lookouts spotted smoke on the horizon.

The *Cuttlefish* abandoned the trawler and went after bigger game. She was in an ideal situation; her batteries were fully charged and she had sighted the vessel a long way off, when there was no chance that it could have spotted her. As the wisp of smoke eventually sharpened into the outline of a ship, the skipper at the periscope saw that he had a major target, a passenger freighter of about ten thousand tons.

"We got in to three thousand yards," Marshall said, "and fired three torpedoes. It was a long wait, so long that we felt sure we had missed, because the time for them to hit passed and nothing happened. But about five seconds later I saw an explosion under the Jap's bow. There was a sheet of flame and a cloud of smoke. Then we heard the sound of the blast. We had been farther away than we thought."

The torpedo also blew up the jinx that had haunted the *Cuttlefish*. The crew were overjoyed. This was more than just an ordinary sinking; it was the first time the elderly submarine had fulfilled the purpose for which she had been built, and it meant a lot to every man on board. The instant the explosion was heard, cheers broke out all over the ship.

Apparently the enemy transport's bow had been opened up. She started spinning rapidly to the right and, when partly turned, ran smack into the second torpedo. That one reversed her course and she started going ahead in the opposite direction and as she turned around a third heavy explosion took place. It was either the third torpedo or an internal blast. Marshall, however, was not going to let anything rob the *Cuttlefish* of victory this time; he edged in and poked a fourth torpedo at the stricken enemy craft.

When the soundman had reported the propeller count on the transport, he had made no mention of a second ship. But a destroyer suddenly emerged from behind the transport and as it started for the submarine down the torpedo track it collided with the fourth torpedo. The submarine came up, and Marshall took a look. The transport was just going under; the destroyer was badly damaged but still afloat, so the submarine cleared the area.

Having at last tasted the pleasant fruit of victory, the Marshall submariners were hungry for another bite. It wasn't long in coming. The *Cuttlefish* was closing the coast about midnight when a destroyer passed nearby. The visibility was poor as the submarine maneuvered to attack the ship, which was on the opposite course. And before she could fire any torpedoes the enemy discovered her. Apparently, there were Japanese submarines in the area too, for the destroyer, instead of driving for the American craft, challenged her. The submarine answered the challenge by diving. The warship made several runs over the *Cuttlefish* but dropped no depth charges, no doubt still believing it might be one of her own boats.

For several long weary days the Americans ranged the coast. Then they sighted some enemy planes and these reported the undersea ship, because soon a destroyer appeared on the scene, plainly on a submarine hunt.

Marshall kept his periscope up and warily watched the Japanese ship. For a moment, it looked as if the destroyer had located him, but then she seemed to have lost him. This was the chance Marshall was waiting for. The *Cuttlefish* attacked and cut loose with two torpedoes, one aimed ahead of the destroyer and the second at the middle of it. The first one ran perfectly, but the target avoided it and swung own the track toward the submarine.

"I could see the crew in whites lined up on deck as lookouts," Marshall said. "And I felt so sure the second torpedo would hit that I stayed at periscope depth. But the second torpedo didn't hit either and we had to go down fast to get out of the way."

Something had gone wrong with the submarine's second torpedo and it had sunk. For a few bad minutes, it looked as if the American submarine would follow it down to the bottom of the sea. She wasn't very deep when the Japanese destroyer churned overhead and dropped the first depth charge. It went off under the bow of the American craft and blew it upward. The submarine started toward the surface at a sharp angle but the diving officer worked fast.

After a hard struggle, he managed to get the ship under control just before she broke water. He took her deep. The Japanese gave the *Cuttlefish* a heavy depth-charging, but her newly acquired good luck held firm and she got away.

Marshall's men were glad to have a breathing spell after the depth-charging, but it lasted too long to suit them. For several days they made no contacts. At last, determined to stir up some action, the captain took his ship close in, to a strait just off a small harbor. For three days and nights she lay there, directly in the path of any traffic that might enter or leave port. Nothing stood in, nothing stood out.

And so on the afternoon of the third day the skipper headed out to sea. Hardly had the Americans got well underway when they saw a big tanker pull in right where they had been lying in ambush only a little while before. The Japanese ship was too far away to attack, but Marshall figured that since she was going into this small port instead of the much larger one up the coast she was in a hurry and would be leaving soon.

The submarine sneaked back and began to patrol the entrance of the harbor. Hour after hour the *Cuttlefish* watched and waited. About one o'clock in the morning the big tanker was sighted coming out.

It was a dark night, with very little moon. The submarine, however, maneuvered to put the target in front of what little moon there was, then remained on the surface and waited. As the tanker loomed nearer and nearer, the Americans topside saw that they had cornered a beautiful prize. The Japanese ship was a whopper. Anxiously wondering whether the lookouts on their victim's bridge could see the black form of the submarine poised for action, the submariners watched the tanker blunder into range.

"Fire one!" the captain ordered.

A little quiver ran along the submarine's keel.

"Fire two!"

"Fire three!"

The torpedo tracks were ghostly lines on the dark water. The grim-faced men on the *Cuttlefish* followed them till they faded into the night. The captain glanced at his watch, waited. Then across the strait came the reverberations of a tremendous explosion. Amidships on the tanker, one torpedo had sent up a mass of flames and a billowing cloud of greenish-yellow smoke.

The vessel spun about and tried to get into port. The *Cuttlefish* was directly in her path and dove quickly to avoid being rammed. Ten minutes later, she poked an inquiring periscope through the surface. The decks of the big tanker were almost awash. Marshall determined to put a final and emphatic period on his ship's achievement. He lined the target up carefully, fired another torpedo. It hit with a thunderous impact; immediately afterwards, a whole series of heavy explosions let go on the Japanese craft.

The submarine's skipper decided they were probably depth charges. It was a farewell salute from the Japanese; the Americans had set it off with the last torpedo they had!

The submarine dove. When she came up a little later, the big Japanese tanker was gone. Captain Marshall not only had broken the jinx on the *Cuttlefish*, but had shown that he could do it again and keep right on doing it.

19 - When Sub Meets Sub

THE SICKENING DRONE OF BOMBERS and torpedo planes filled the air over Pearl Harbor. An ugly pall of smoke was rising toward the sky as the raiders found their targets. Treachery and destruction, plotted in Japan, shattered the peace of half the world.

As the enemy aircraft roared in from the sea, the torpedo planes were obliged to swoop low to drop their deadly missiles, aimed at our battlewagons, lying at anchor in Battleship Row. What's more, they had to sweep past the base, where several of our submarines were tied up. From the submarines, deck and machine guns blazed away at the flying enemy. One of our submarines was the second ship in the harbor to open fire on the raiders.

Manning her after machine gun was Torpedoman Second Class Mignone. He sent burst after burst of bullets at the torpedo planes winging past the ship's fantail. A defiant Japanese skimmed low, his long torpedo plainly visible beneath the fuselage of his plane. Mignone got the Japanese plane in his sights, and the machine gun spat furiously. Slugs tore into the plane; it exploded and plunged into the water in a mass of flames.

Some of those who witnessed this unusual feat, a submarine knocking down an enemy plane, expressed the belief that Mignone had hit the warhead of the torpedo and exploded it. At any rate, the after-end of the torpedo was later recovered from the bottom of the harbor, indicating that the torpedo had been exploded. A destroyer which was moored nearby also accounted for one of the Nipponese raiders that tried to run the gantlet and plant a torpedo in the big warships ahead.

The submarine that drew the first Japanese blood for our undersea fleet by bringing down an airplane was the USS *Tautog*, skippered by Commander Joseph H. Willingham, Jr. She had pulled into port only two days earlier, after a forty-five-day training patrol, and most of the officers and men were at a rest camp that Sunday morning.

Only one officer was near at hand, living at the bachelors' quarters at the submarine base, but Willingham saw the planes come over and raced from town back to his ship. He arrived only fifteen or twenty minutes after the attack started. Joe Willingham of Pell City, Alabama, was graduated from the Naval Academy in 1926. Incidentally, a *tautog*, or blackfish, is a food fish of the Atlantic coast of the United States. It was the submarine *Tautog* that, during aerial bomb training before the war, emerged from the depths with an unexploded practice bomb resting on her top deck.

Willingham's big fleet submarine, having received her baptism of fire, pulled out from Pearl Harbor within a few days of the raid. Her destination was the Japan-mandated Marshall Islands. Willingham's orders called for a complete reconnaissance. Any Japanese ships he could sink in the process would be all to the good, of course. The *Tautog* had a pretty rough time, according to her captain, with Japanese planes driving her under and enemy patrol ships repeatedly dumping their ashcans on the spot they imagined she was occupying.

But her mission was accomplished successfully. When the *Tautog* returned, Willingham brought back data on the Japanese outposts that subsequently proved of great value. He also had received credit for damaging an enemy ship with a torpedo. The submarine was able to get in only one attack, on a minelayer; she scored a hit but planes drove her under before she could see the target sink.

During this patrol, the *Tautog* submariners had one heartbreaking experience. Three Japanese submarines were sighted coming in on the surface, but it was so foggy and the visibility was so bad, that the American ship couldn't attack. The glimpse of those enemy submarines, however, must have been an omen; the next time Joe Willingham's craft encountered a Japanese submarine it was a different story.

After the scouting patrol, the *Tautog* was inactive for several weeks, while she underwent a navy yard refit, but at last to the great joy of her crew she got underway. Once more she headed for Japan-mandated islands, although this time it was the Carolines, farther west, which included the powerful mystery base on Truk.

The submarine was only two days out of Pearl Harbor. The officer of the deck, as the big *Tautog* hauled westward on the surface about ten o'clock in the morning, was Lieutenant Jim Barnard, a man with the eyes of an eagle. Barnard, scanning the tumbling expanse of ocean ahead, caught a brief, dazzling glint. He knew instantly what it was—the reflection of the sun in the window of a periscope.

From that moment on, the lurking enemy's position was never lost, for she kept her periscope up and obviously was trying to get into position to attack Willingham's submarine.

The second Barnard saw the reflection on the sea he called for battle stations and ordered the tubes made ready. By the time Willingham arrived on the bridge the Japanese submarine was on the port bow. And it was at this point that the quick-thinking American submariners outwitted their enemy. They swung the surfaced submarine hard right, giving the Japanese the impression that the *Tautog* was trying to get away. Actually, she was attacking. Willingham steadied the ship and fired a torpedo quickly—from a stern tube. It was offhand shooting.

"We waited and waited," Willingham said, "and had just about given up when we saw the water heave upward. A ball of yellowish smoke arose. We knew it was from a warhead. The smoke is a distinctive color, and once you've seen it, you can't mistake it."

The attack on the Japanese submarine was all over in less than two minutes. The *Tautog* made contact with an American patrol plane, which circled over the enormous oil slick, the cork and other debris on the surface of the ocean.

"That pilot just kept flying around and around over the spot where the periscope had been," Willingham said.

"We found out afterwards that he was so interested in looking at what had happened that he didn't want to leave. But finally he flew over us and signaled: 'Congratulations! You got him!' "

Barnard was awarded the Silver Star for spotting the enemy ship. The *Tautog* continued on to the area of her patrol, where a concentration of enemy forces had been reported.

She sighted her first ship there about dawn. The enemy craft was darkened, but the submarine made a good approach and was on the point of firing when Willingham saw in the increasing light that it was a Japanese hospital ship. He couldn't understand why she was darkened, instead of carrying a lighted red cross and running lights as required by international rules, but he held his fire.

A couple of days later, however, the submarine encountered another enemy vessel just at dawn, and this time it was different. This ship was a freighter of about ten thousand tons—a tidy target—and the submarine poked a spread of torpedoes at her. One of them smashed into the big cargo ship, but she ran groggily for shore and managed to beach herself. Later, however, the submarine saw her again; she had washed off the beach and sunk.

At that season the area of the *Tautog*'s patrol had almost as much fog and poor visibility as the Aleutians. The Americans seldom sighted a ship before it was almost on top of them, which was pretty nerve-racking. For instance, a few days after sinking the 10,000-ton cargo ship, a division of four destroyers standing in from the Solomons suddenly loomed out of the mist. The submarine ducked, and the four enemy warships roared right over her. The Willingham craft ran to the west for several days in an effort to intercept a carrier believed to be in the vicinity, but saw no sign of her and after wasting five days on this errand, she returned to her station.

At the end of World War I, the Allies gathered around the peace table at Versailles unwittingly dealt Japan a handful of aces in the Pacific Ocean. For her small part in the struggle they gave her a mandate over numerous islands, the strategic importance of which was overlooked then but was all too well understood twenty-four years later.

Under the terms of the mandate, Japan was not to fortify the islands but that meant less than nothing to the treacherous Nipponese. As soon as the Japanese took them over they barred foreigners from many of the islands, and in almost no time were constructing what they imagined were impregnable bases.

When the mantle of deceit was cast aside in December 1941, it was Japan's boast that no alien eyes had ever gazed on a certain one of these islands since she had commanded it. This was the island of Truk. It lay in the area of Commander Willingham's patrol, so he decided to break the taboo and take a good look at this mystery base. He moved in toward the beach. The Japanese had plenty of patrols, both far at sea and around the entrances to the lagoon, and after brushes with a couple of these antisubmarine craft, the *Tautog* about four o'clock one afternoon slipped right up next to the reef around the lagoon, poked up her periscope and looked over.

While Willingham was satisfying his curiosity and noting important details about the island citadel, he sighted a large ship standing out of one of the channels. About twenty minutes later, a second, smaller ship followed her. The submarine was not in a position to attack, but the two enemy vessels obviously were worth her attention, so she headed away from the lagoon.

The Americans were in luck—the bigger of the ships was steaming back and forth, waiting for the other to catch up with her. Then the two made their rendezvous and waited around a little while before setting out on their course. It gave the *Tautog* time enough to draw near and determine that one of them was a cargo ship of about ten thousand tons and the other a fast, heavily armed converted freighter of about four thousand tons, acting as escort.

The chase began. The submarine surfaced and kept the Japanese ships just barely in sight, yet stayed far enough away so that no one aboard them was likely to spot her. Willingham gradually maneuvered his ship ahead of the two targets until he was in a good position to attack. This time submerged and his periscope down, he made a sound shot. There was one hit; a terrific explosion took place on the bigger vessel.

"After that, it was just like the Fourth of July," Willingham said. "There were fireworks all over. We had put a torpedo in a big ammunition ship."

The Nipponese vessel blew herself to pieces. Her escort charged the submarine and kept her down a couple of hours by depth charges; but finally the Yanks shook off the Japanese and headed toward Australia. They had sharp eyes in Willingham's ship. Barnard picked up the glint of the Japanese periscope in the sunlight; Lieutenant Commander Carmick, the second officer, first saw a faint puff of smoke on the horizon, and a little later the masts of the *Tautog*'s next target. It was late in the afternoon as the enemy vessel came into full view of the submarine, which had been maneuvered ahead of her.

The ship, a big slow-moving troopship, was all alone, with no sign of an escort. The Americans fired two torpedoes. The first passed in front of the target, which was moving even slower than Willingham estimated. But the second "pickle" crashed into her just forward of the bridge.

"The foremast went four feet straight up in the air," the submarine's captain related. "She sank in five minutes." At sundown, as the Japanese transport slipped beneath the waves, troops were still clinging all over her and frantically trying to launch lifeboats and rafts. The submarine's crew came topside and watched her go down.

After the *Tautog* had reached Australia, Lieutenant Commander "Hutch" Hutchinson ran into her captain. Hutch had been skipper on another submarine, which had followed the same course as Willingham's about a week later.

"Did you sink a ship on the way down at such and such a spot?" Hutch asked, giving Joe Willingham the location.

Willingham nodded.

"Was it a troop transport?"

Again the submarine captain nodded. "Yes."

"Well!" Hutch exclaimed. "When we got there, thousands of dead Japs were floating around in the water with their feet sticking up!"

Willingham received a Navy Cross and a gold star in Australia. They were for different patrols, but presented at the same time.

On her next time out the submarine sank one Japanese ship, a tender. She picked up a couple of others, two of the finest vessels in Tokyo's merchant fleet, but was obliged to let them fade over the horizon without firing a shot. First the submarine trailed a large *maru*, which, just as the Americans were about to start an approach, turned on a red cross in lights. Willingham let her go. On the heels of the hospital ship, a beautiful liner appeared. But she carried her identification—she was the ship that was evacuating Allied diplomats from Japan. The submarine had been expecting her, but she was not on schedule when sighted.

"They were fine big Japanese ships," Willingham said wistfully.

On her next patrol the *Tautog* was ordered off the Philippines. She had just gone through Sibutu Pass when she spotted a ship in a rain squall and dove. After the rain let up, she could see that her target was a small one, so she surfaced. A couple of rounds from the deck gun brought the enemy to a halt. It was a hundred-foot diesel fishing boat. Besides thirty-two Nipponese, the Americans saw four Filipinos on board. They later learned that it was a Filipino boat which the enemy had seized.

Willingham called out to the Islanders, "Want to come with us?"

That was all the Filipinos needed. They jumped into the sea and swam to the submarine as fast as they could, which wasn't very fast because they were in such terrible physical condition. Their Japanese captors had forced them into virtual slavery, never allowing them ashore and feeding them barely enough to keep them alive. "Those Filipinos were certainly glad to see us," Willingham said. "They were bruised from beatings they had received and were thin and emaciated. Besides that, they were suffering from scurvy and had ugly-looking sores on their legs. The only clothing the Japs had let them have was so filthy that we threw it over the side. After we had washed them up, doctored them and dressed their sores, they spent the next couple of days just eating and sleeping."

The Japanese on the fishing craft were ordered to pull away in their four small boats. Then the submariners had some target practice; they sank the enemy ship with gunfire. A couple of days later, they heard a Tokyo broadcast lamenting the cruelty and inhumanity of American submarines toward those aboard the ships they attacked.

"Actually," said Willingham, "we gave those Japs in their small boats food and water and their course to land. They were near shore and could make it easily."

The four Filipinos provided the crew of the submarine with much entertainment during the patrol. One of them was a former ship's steward and another a first-class baker.

They stayed in the Navy; it happened this way: When Willingham was in Australia, Admiral Lockwood, at that time Commander of Submarines, Southwest Pacific, had mentioned to him that the restrictions against Filipinos as messboys in the Navy had been removed. Then the Admiral had added jokingly, "Bring me back some messboys."

After the Filipinos were rescued, Joe Willingham sent a message to Admiral Lockwood: "Your four messboys are on board." The only other major excitement of the patrol was a typhoon which the *Tautog* battled for five days, during which she was able only with the greatest difficulty to keep from being blown into the reef-filled "dangerous ground" west of Palawan. At the end of her patrol, Willingham's ship headed for Pearl Harbor. After arriving there Willingham said good-bye to his officers and crew. He had been ordered to return to new construction in the United States. It was November 28, 1942, and that is the date inscribed on one of the finest gold watches in the Navy, one which Joe Willingham prizes highly. It was presented to him by the officers and crew of the submarine he had commanded so long and with such conspicuous success in the war zone.

Young Joe, his son, age fourteen, also received a present from the crew of his father's submarine, and he valued it just as much as his dad did the watch. It was a blue battle flag, which the submariners made especially for him. In the middle was the twin dolphin insignia of the Submarine Service. At the top was a bomb with wings, to represent the torpedo plane shot down in the raid on Pearl Harbor. And down each side was a total of seven Japanese flags, both battle and merchant, standing for the ships the *Tautog* was officially credited with sinking. Five of those flags represented a total of forty-five thousand tons of Japan's shipping, an average of nine thousand tons per ship. "Get the big ones first!"

During all the time they spent at sea, probably the greatest satisfaction of all for the officers and men of the *Tautog* came from two attacks they made in the course of their second patrol, off Truk. These attacks took place the day after the submarine had just barely ducked under the division of Japanese destroyers in the fog.

Again the weather was hazy and the visibility poor, as the big American submarine picked up a Japanese submarine standing in on the surface. It was a tempting sight. The enemy submarine was flying a large battle flag, flaming with a red sun and red rays on its white background. Besides that she was painted up like a billboard, with huge numbers and another battle flag on her conning tower. But the Americans watched her draw away, because they couldn't get into a position for an attack.

Willingham, however, followed the enemy submarine's track and about an hour later along came another. Her battle flag also was fluttering proudly in the breeze. The Yankee commander eyed her coldly as he maneuvered the *Tautog*. This time he was ready and lined her up carefully.

Then came the order to fire one torpedo. It exploded with a roar in the double hull of the enemy ship.

"I'm certain that we sank her," Willingham said, "although we were only credited with damaging her, because we didn't see her go down. She got out of visibility."

The American commander had proved he could deal with enemy submarines both under the sea and on top of it. He had sunk his first Japanese submarine while the *Tautog* was on the surface and the target submerged; he had slammed a torpedo into a second one while the target was on the surface and the *Tautog* was submerged. And he hadn't finished yet.

Down the alley, right in the path of the other two Japanese submarines, came a third one, battle flags flying. Willingham could hardly believe his eyes, and his men were ready to explode with excitement and delight as the word spread. The submarine drove steadily onward. Willingham gave the order to fire. A warhead slammed into another Japanese submarine and stopped her cold.

She was sinking slowly as her crew spewed out topside and started to abandon ship. Carefully Willingham's fighter closed the target. Another torpedo jumped from the *Tautog*'s bow. It smacked into the Japanese submarine with a shattering explosion. Down she went.

20 – A Dream Comes True

THE OFFICER OF THE DECK, Lieutenant Walter Allen Sharer, had been out of the Naval Academy less than four years. He was sound and communications officer on the big fleet submarine. Both he and his ship, the USS *Salmon*, had been commissioned in the same year—1938. The responsibility for the submarine was in the hands of the slender young lieutenant as he peered into the darkness.

But he had plenty of assistance in scanning the tumbling water around him. Three lookouts and Tim Wood, quartermaster, were on the bridge. Wood was noted for his keen eyesight—a good man to have topside when you're sneaking your ship into an area where an enemy convoy of more than a hundred ships has been reported. In the convoy were transports, warships and a carrier. The *Salmon* had been told to go in and get the carrier. It was a large order.

The night was black as pitch, with neither moon nor stars, as the submarine drove ahead on the surface toward Lingayen Gulf, on Luzon. Nevertheless, the sharp-eyed men on the bridge from time to time made out hazy shapes going in the opposite direction. They concluded that these were transports, although at the distance and in the darkness it was impossible to identify them accurately. In any event, the submarine was in no position to attack.

Then the lookouts noticed two of these ghostly ships much closer, moving swiftly on the opposite course. They were destroyers, which drew aft and continued on their way. Presently, however, one of the lookouts observed that they had swung around and were following. Sharer promptly ordered the tubes made ready. The captain, Lieutenant Commander E. B. McKinney, and the executive officer, Lieutenant I. S. Hartman, appeared on the bridge. Hartman manned the phones. The skipper didn't have time to adjust his eyes to the extreme darkness, and so it was up to Sharer to direct the attack.

The enemy ships came up portside in a column until they were nearly abeam. Sharer, who had his night glasses trained on them, changed the submarine's course to the right about ninety degrees, leaving the Japanese astern. Then for a few minutes the Americans lost sight of the destroyers but almost immediately picked them up again. There were the two enemy craft, dead astern and still heading for the submarine. With Sharer at the binoculars giving orders, Tim Wood, at the wheel, got a good setup.

The youthful officer of the deck waited coolly until the targets were only about seven hundred yards away, then fired two torpedoes. One of the destroyers had started to turn. The first torpedo caught her about two-thirds of the way back from the bow, evidently in the boiler room. The explosion was not only thunderous but dazzling. A tremendous flare leaped skyward and lit up the entire area. It momentarily blinded the men on the bridge of the undersea fighter, and it also blew the Japanese ship all to pieces. From the after-torpedo room came word that two torpedo explosions had been heard. The next day our Navy planes reported that two destroyers were missing from the group that had been there the previous day. There was no doubt about the one enemy ship and it seemed as if they had bagged the second, but the blast had been too bright for them to see.

The submarine dove and took a brief depth-charging from the second destroyer; if it was hit, at least it did not go down immediately.

Having finished off one of Japan's warships with brilliant fireworks, the submarine pushed on toward Lingayen Gulf.

After a while she surfaced. From the soundman came a report of screws dead ahead. The eyes of the officers and lookouts on the bridge tried to pierce the gloom. But no one could see anything. Finally, Sharer made out a dim shape headed toward them, a little on the port bow. The others still were unable to distinguish it. Suddenly Sharer let out a yell.

"Look out, she's dead ahead!"

The men topside dived for the conning-tower hatch as the *Salmon* started a dive for her life. Her course met that of the onrushing warship, but fortunately on a different level. Submerged, the undersea craft ran the length of the enemy's keel. The Japanese knew she was there, too, because they dumped over some depth charges, but McKinney and his men kept right on going and soon evaded the enemy. From time to time, they picked up screw beats on the sound gear, but it was decided not to go any farther into the gulf. Instead, the submarine cleared the area.

The destroyer she had just sunk was the *Salmon*'s first victim and won for her skipper the Navy Cross. Sharer eventually received the Silver Star for his part in the sinking, as well as for his outstanding work as communications officer on later patrols. Hartman left the ship at the end of the second patrol, and took command of an S-boat, with which he soon covered himself with glory by sinking a Japanese submarine and a cruiser.

When war began in the Pacific, McKinney's submarine was anchored in Manila Bay. She spent December 9 sitting on the bottom. About four days later, she started off on her first patrol toward Lingayen Gulf. When she cleared that area after sinking the destroyer, McKinney received orders to proceed south. The *Salmon* patrolled down through the Philippines as far as the waters below the island of Amboina and the Molucca Sea. On the way, she saw nothing of any Japanese ships. But on a small island west of Amboina, she picked up some smoke rising from a little bay and went over to investigate it. It was a false alarm, and when the skipper looked back through the periscope, he saw a convoy steaming through the strait the submarine had just left. That was a blow.

That night, the undersea ship started into Amboina Bay. The entrance is only about one thousand yards wide, flanked with cliffs. It is like a corridor. The submarine no sooner had poked her nose into this narrow passage, which is about a mile long, than two enemy destroyers appeared standing out. The *Salmon* was on the surface, and the enemy quickly spotted her. The Japanese were so excited that they began to dump their ashcans even before she dove. The Americans got out as fast as possible and managed to evade their pursuers.

The *Salmon* wound up her patrol at Tjilatjap (the sailors called it Tell-a-Jap) on the south coast of Java. She had been at sea sixty-seven days. Toward the end the men aboard her were receiving the minimum food allowance. This was one of the times when submariners were not the best fed of anyone in the Navy. While the ship was being worked on in port, Javanese natives were given the job of painting her. They swung their brushes with great zest, but without much discretion.

On the second day in Tell-a-Jap, half the crew were sent to a rest camp. They needed a rest, but they didn't get it. The morning after they arrived at the camp, word came to return to their ship as fast as possible. The submarine had orders to get underway.

The second patrol of the *Salmon* was in the Java Sea. Probably no ship in the war operated under more trying circumstances. In addition to the fact that the shallow water was teeming with enemy warcraft on a perpetual hunt for submarines, the American submarine was only a few days out when her air conditioning broke down. For the rest of the patrol, the temperature inside her was above a hundred nearly all the time. It was almost unbearable for the crew, who were still tired out from their previous patrol, but they had to bear it.

Their first attack took place at night, while the *Salmon* was running on the surface. There was a bright moon. The officer of the deck sighted what appeared to be a cruiser coming toward them almost dead ahead. The submarine held her course till she was so close that there was a chance the lookouts on the warship might spot her, then she dove. Using her periscope, she maneuvered to attack. She lined up the cruiser and fired two torpedoes at her. Two explosions followed. But the *Salmon* had to dive to escape a depth-charging by a destroyer that was accompanying the cruiser. The destroyer came tearing down the torpedo tracks and began dumping her ashcans. McKinney managed to get out from under; a little later he brought his ship up and looked around. Neither the cruiser nor the destroyer was in sight. On the records, the submarine is credited with damaging the former.

In reading about operations of our submarine fleet, it must always be remembered that no ship was scored as sunk unless she was seen to go down or the evidence that she did was beyond question. If the torpedo explosion was heard but the submarine was forced under by escort vessels and depth bombs and unable to see what happened above, she got credit for damaging the target. Undoubtedly a good many of these "damaged" craft sank, or at least were forced into port for some time for repairs.

From the night McKinney's submarine hit the cruiser until the end of her patrol, she was kept busy dodging the Japanese destroyers that were combing the whole area. On one occasion she was running on the surface at night when the lookouts picked up one large and two small shapes on the starboard bow. Before the submarine could continue her investigations, a searchlight suddenly cut through the night from one of the enemy craft. It came to rest directly on the submarine's bridge. Times Square at night in peacetime isn't any brighter. The *Salmon* flipped her fins and made a quick dive, as the two smaller shapes materialized into destroyers bearing down on her.

She managed to evade the depth charges and as soon as the captain dared he eased the submarine to the surface and sent out a contact report. As a result, another of our undersea fighters managed to pick up the Japanese task force and attack it.

When the *Salmon* was driven under on another occasion her outboard water exhaust valves failed to close entirely. This was a dangerous accident for a submarine. With enemy depth bombs zip-booming around her, she was compelled to use all her pumps to keep from flooding. But the rugged submariners who had been sticking it out on patrol with no air conditioning and the inside of their ship like a bake oven, managed to get away and bring the *Salmon* to the surface undamaged.

The lack of rest between patrols, the constant hammering by the Japanese antisubmarine patrol, and the distressing conditions aboard the ship finally wore the men down physically and mentally. The captain was obliged to send a message reporting that the crew exhaustion had become serious. He was ordered to proceed to Fremantle, Australia.

It was the end of March. For the first time, Sharer learned that while he was sinking the destroyer off Lingayen Gulf on December 23, things were getting ready to happen on his home front in far-off Coronado, California. At Fremantle, he received a letter from his wife and also a telegram. They both contained the same news. His second son had been born on Christmas Day. It was a year to a day, however, after the sinking of the destroyer before Sharer saw the youngster. From Fremantle, the *Salmon* moved around the southwest corner of Australia and into Albany on the south coast for a badly needed overhaul. The ship stayed in port three weeks, but the officers and crew remained aboard and worked on her.

Incidentally, few if any of our submarine officers exceeded the record for continuous service which Sharer and McKinney established. Their ship finally pulled into Pearl Harbor on December 7, 1942, exactly one year after the Japanese dropped the bombs there that plunged us into war. In all that time, neither Sharer nor his captain had even one day of leave. Except for occasional visits ashore for a few hours, they remained on their ship. They made five patrols and sank some of Japan's finest warships and cargo vessels.

Liberty, however, was granted the submariners as often as possible in Australia and both officers and men were royally entertained by the Australians.

"They treated us fine," Sharer said. "They had all of us at their homes for meals. They gave dances for us. I don't believe American sailors ever have been treated better than the men on our ship were in Australia."

After her third patrol the *Salmon* put into Albany again, and this time the men were sent to a rest camp. But the officers got no day off; they stayed on the ship and continued the overhauling with a relief crew. On this visit, however, the officers and men repaid their generous hosts to some extent. The ship gave a big party.

The *Salmon's* fourth patrol was her least eventful. She proceeded to Palawan Passage and Balibac Strait, east of the dangerous ground, where she spent many days and sighted only one ship. The attack on this failed; the torpedoes missed, and the ship got away.

Her time up, the submarine headed for Fremantle. As she was coming into Australia she ran into heavy weather. Two huge waves swept over the bridge and poured down into the conning tower, where the water was knee deep. The hatch was slammed shut. With a lot of the electrical equipment grounded out, communication was cut off and for a few minutes they had a bad time on board. The men on the bridge thought those below were lost; the men below believed the submariners topside were goners.

About the middle of October, McKinney shoved off on his fifth patrol, off the Philippines. The *Salmon* arrived in her area, from Manila up to Lingayen, before she clashed with the enemy. One day, while running on the surface, the mast of a ship was sighted on the port quarter, although the ship itself was well over the horizon. One of the officers stood on top of the periscope shears—bracing legs— and clung to the periscope in order to get a better view. From this relatively lofty perch he continued to pick up other masts, until he had a total of nine ships spotted. Six of them, apparently, were cargo ships and the other three destroyer escorts.

The officer drew a diagram of the formation he thought the convoy was in and passed it down for the captain to see. It was decided that the six freighters were in two parallel columns of three each, with the destroyers buzzing around them. It was a pretty set up for the submarine. She changed her course so that the two columns would pass on either side of her, and moved in to attack. Before the enemy was close enough to spot her, she dove.

The unsuspecting Japanese ships plowed onward toward the waiting submarine, whose battle periscope was an almost invisible fly spec on the surface of the South China Sea. One column of freighters came toward her on the starboard and the other on the portside. The *Salmon* turned right and headed toward the first ship in the left-hand column. All tubes were made ready but only two were fired.

The periscope was down while the torpedoes were on their way, but within the submarine the men heard one of them explode. McKinney poked his periscope up for a quick look. Instantly he ordered the ship to go deep. The second cargo vessel was about to ram her.

By this time, the destroyers were milling around dropping depth charges. The Americans tried to get outside the formation of enemy ships, but they were heard and had to give up the idea. Finally the entire convoy passed overhead. The submarine fired no more torpedoes; at that point she was only concerned with getting away. The soundman heard the Japanese freighter breaking up and on the records McKinney's ship is credited with sinking her.

The next convoy the prowling submarine came across was almost identical in make-up. Once again, the *Salmon* successfully maneuvered into a position between and at right angles to the oncoming columns of freighters. As before, all tubes were made ready, but this time the submarine really let the enemy have it. Three forward tubes were fired at the lead ship in the left-hand column and one at the second ship. From the stern, two torpedoes started toward the second ship in the other column.

For a few minutes a regular school of tin fish was churning up the water inside the lines of the convoy. Then, after the calculated run of time, they began to explode in Japanese hulls. Four distinct blasts were heard by the anxiously waiting men in the submarine. They also heard other explosions, easily identified as the destroyers opened a depth-charge attack. At his listening gear, the soundman caught the welcome crackling noise of sinking ships breaking up when the pressure of the water crushes them. Officially, the submarine was credited with one tanker sunk and one freighter and one tanker damaged. She evaded the depth charges and made a successful getaway.

On two different nights, during this patrol, the Americans sighted enemy hospital ships and watched them slip into the darkness toward Japan. In accordance with regulations, they were carrying illuminated red crosses and port and starboard running lights.

One of these hospital ships was sighted on a very dark night. Suddenly ahead of her and astern of the submarine, another ship turned on running lights for about thirty seconds. A hospital ship was one thing to the *Salmon*'s officers, the second vessel was another. They headed in to make an approach and tried to pick up the enemy craft, which by now had turned out her lights. They failed to find her, nor could sound catch the churning of screws, except those of the hospital ship. It was a mystery target so far as the submarine ever knew; a ghost ship that was swallowed by the night.

The next attack on a Japanese craft was carried out more in the tradition of the privateers of John Paul Jones's day than according to usual methods of a modern submarine.

The *Salmon* was on the surface at night when she spotted a fair-sized spitkit seemingly engaged in fishing.

The ship had a shaded light, which was visible to those aboard the submarine. McKinney, on the bridge, hailed the other ship. At that the spitkit started her engines and began to move away, and her crew began to heave things overboard. A few bursts from the submarine's machine gun into her engine room brought the spitkit to a halt. The sea was rough, but the submarine ran alongside and tied up to the vessel.

A boarding party consisting of Lieutenant L. E. Davis, the gunnery officer, and Lieutenant (j.g.) T. B. Denegre leaped to the deck of the spitkit. Davis was wielding a large bowie knife and Denegre had a forty-five. They must have looked terrifying, for as they headed for the engine room, a Japanese popped out and dove into the water.

Denegre moved forward on the portside. Then the men on his own ship shouted that a couple of Japanese were lying down on the starboard side of the hatch, so he sneaked around and started for the two. They leaped toward him. The forty-five barked a few times, and Japan had two less sailors in her navy. All the other Japanese had gone over the side by this time.

On one of the dead Japanese was an expensive American wristwatch, which evidently had been taken from somebody in Manila. Other articles found on the spitkit included a chronometer, radio equipment, and nine Japanese passports for the crew. All the pictures on them had been taken with the men in the uniform of the Japanese Navy, although aboard the sampan none of them were in uniform. That put them in the category of spies. Denegre and Davis doused the sampan with torpedo alcohol and set it afire. It burned for about two hours and then exploded as the flames reached its fuel supply.

As a matter of fact, there was a third and uninvited member of the boarding party. He was a Filipino messboy who formerly had been a Filipino Scout—and how he hated Japanese! Without orders, he followed Denegre and Davis. His only weapon was a pocket knife. But he was unlucky. He tripped over one of the enemy Denegre had shot and fell flat on his face. By the time he picked himself up, there were no Japanese around.

Weeks later, when the *Salmon* arrived in Pearl Harbor, the officers and men read with great amusement an article reprinted from the New York Times in a paper there. It described the sinking of the spitkit as told over the Japanese radio.

The announcer said a sampan had been attacked and boarded by American submarine officers, wearing beards and smoking big black cigars. They had destroyed everybody aboard. Aside from the fact that the details were mostly incorrect, it was hard to understand where the Tokyo radio got all the details if everybody aboard had been killed. Actually, the spitkit had been fairly close to the beach, and the Japanese who went overboard, if they were good swimmers, had a pretty fair chance of reaching shore.

It was on a patrol off the coast of French Indo-China in May 1942, that McKinney did what every submarine captain hopes to do sometime during his career. In this case it won the captain a gold star in lieu of a second Navy Cross.

The patrol began auspiciously. The *Salmon* was hunting the enemy back and forth across the South China Sea when, at night, she picked up the dark smudge of a freighter. Speeding along on the surface, the submarine headed the target off and began her approach. As soon as the other ship was nicely lined up, the submarine launched two torpedoes. Then two explosions, one after another, were plainly heard aboard the submarine.

Immediately the cargo vessel began to list, but in an effort to make sure of her, McKinney swung his craft around and fired a torpedo from a stern tube. It missed, but by this time the freighter was going under. It was a successful attack but there were better ones to come. The *Salmon* was in an active section of the ocean.

Enemy destroyers were patrolling up and down the sea lanes, attempting to guard the materials which Japan was sending to the fighting fronts or hauling back from the lands she had seized and was looting. One day the *Salmon* caught one of the destroyers sitting motionless on the surface. It looked like a pushover.

The attacking submarine managed to approach to about twelve hundred yards from her squatting target, but the position was unfavorable for firing torpedoes. Just then the destroyer got underway, heading directly for the *Salmon*. The American ship promptly ducked, and the destroyer passed overhead. But she dropped no depth charges and the submariners, braced for the zip-boom of ashcans which never came, concluded that the destroyer hadn't spotted them after all and her course straight for them had been only coincidence. It was a few nights later that the *Salmon*'s biggest prize hove into sight. The submarine was on the surface; about four miles away one of the lookouts picked up a heavy cruiser, heading toward them off the port bow. Instantly, the submarine's course was altered to meet the oncoming target. When the distance between them had closed sufficiently, the undersea ship dove and maneuvered to attack.

Sharp-eyed Tim Wood was making the observations, and as the enemy drew closer he reported that the big warship was escorted by two destroyers on the port and starboard quarters.

Excitement was running high in the submarine after word spread that they had a top-flight target. McKinney ordered four bow tubes made ready. The Americans waited. On and on rushed the cruiser and her twin escorts. Finally, she was only one thousand yards away and broadside to the submarine, which was poised for a kill. McKinney gave orders to fire all four tubes.

Moments later, at evenly spaced intervals, like the blows of a mammoth pile driver, came four terrific explosions.

Everyone in the submarine could hear them plainly; cheers rang out all over the ship. At the periscope, McKinney watched his torpedoes hit—one after another—right where they were aimed. The first one caught the cruiser on the bow. The next two crashed into her amidships, and the final explosion tore her stern wide open. Four torpedoes, four hits.

The big Japanese warship shuddered from bow to stern, and sank out of sight in record time. It was a submarine commander's fondest dream come true.

21 – Submarine Warfare

THE FIRST JAPANESE SHIP SUNK BY an American submarine was the 8,633-ton *Atsutasan Maru*. She was sent to the bottom by the USS *Swordfish* in an attack off Hainan Island on December 15, 1941—when the war was eight days old. The last sinkings of enemy craft were on August 14, 1945, the day on which Japan announced that she would accept the peace terms drawn up at the Potsdam conference of the United States, Great Britain and Russia.

On that date the submarine *Torsky* sank two destroyer escorts; a few hours earlier the *Spikefish* had bagged a Japanese submarine. In the forty-four months between those two dates, our undersea fleet piled up a record of enemy sinkings that, in looking back, is almost beyond belief. According to the official Navy summary of the results obtained by our submarines, a total of 1,944 major Japanese vessels were sunk.

Of this number, 194 were warships and 1,750 were steel merchant ships. These totals do not include the hundreds of lesser craft destroyed, nor do they take into account the many enemy ships damaged more or less severely, on which no accurate count could well be made. Japan's total loss of naval vessels is placed at 412, with an additional 272 small craft destroyed. Since these losses are credited to all arms of our services—air, surface and undersea—the record of the Submarine Service becomes increasingly impressive.

The warship bag of our submarines was divided as follows: 1 battleship, 8 aircraft carriers, 15 cruisers, 42 destroyers, 28 submarines, and 100 lesser naval vessels. At no time were there more than 50,000 men in the submarine branch of our Navy. But the operations of our underwater ships took the lives of 276,000 of the enemy, more than five for every man in the submarines. Approximately 105,000 Japanese civilians, 71,000 Navy personnel, and 100,000 Army personnel were drowned or otherwise killed by submarine action.

The scoreboard tells the story of the magnificent part our undersea fleet played in victory. But it was not achieved without cost. We paid for it with the lives of 3,505 of our gallant submariners, officers and men—one American life for every seventy-nine Japanese killed. We finished the war with 240 submarines, 199 of them the latest fleet type. Our losses were 52 ships, although seven of these were due to accidents or intentional destruction to keep the submarines from falling into enemy hands. As a general thing, when a submarine is sunk, all on board perish, but at least some of the personnel on six of our lost submarines survived. Eleven officers and 157 men were recovered from prison camps after they had been rescued following the sinking of the *S-44, Grenadier, Perch, Sculpin, Tullibee* and *Tautog*.

At the end of the war, Japan had 51 submarines, not counting a number of two-man midget submarines she had built, which proved to be an ineffectual and negligible factor in the submarine warfare. One of them ran aground just outside Pearl Harbor following the Japanese attack and the lieutenant commanding it was captured. We knew about them early.

After the surrender, our occupation forces in Japan destroyed an undisclosed number of a novel type of undersea weapon. This was described as "the underwater cousin of the Kamikaze suicide bomber." It was a midget submarine that was given the name "Kaiten," meaning 'great storm.' The Kaitens were built in two sizes—an eight-ton model operated by one man and an eighteen-ton model to carry a crew of two. The former was used against American shipping "without definite results," and the latter was still in the experimental stage when the war ended.

According to Vice-Admiral Tamura, the one-man submarines were launched from the deck of a large submarine while still submerged. The operator—a volunteer or draftee suicide—entered the tiny ship through a special hatch from the mother submarine, which could carry as many as six of these unique missiles on deck. They had explosive-packed warheads and a range of thirty miles at low speed or twelve miles at top speed. These "human torpedoes," Admiral Tamura said, were first used at Palau and Saipan.

The Nipponese, however, did not limit their submarine experiments to undersize craft. They built seven or eight 3,000-ton submarines, the I-14 class, which carried two airplanes in a deck hangar, and a couple of 5,500-ton undersea ships, the I-400 and I-401, which could carry four planes on their decks. These larger ones were easily the biggest submarines ever built by anyone. Both were seized after Japan capitulated, along with one of the smaller carrier submarines, all the others of this class having been lost.

Our Navy, however, doesn't think much of submarine aircraft carriers. As Vice-Admiral Charles A. Lockwood, top submarine commander in the Pacific during the last years of the conflict, expressed it, the idea is futile because they could not possibly carry enough planes to make an attack effective. On the other hand, our Navy was very much interested in learning how the two bigger Japanese submarines managed to attain an underwater speed of thirteen knots. Also in captured blueprints of a proposed German ship capable of twenty-five knots submerged. Vice-Admiral Lockwood, incidentally, declared that he would favor submarines as carriers for our new-type rocket bombs. But he also said he thought that our present 1,500-ton submarines are the ideal size. Bigger ships are bigger targets.

The exploits of our underwater ships and the heroism of the men who manned them covered such a vast field that it is impossible for a single volume to do more than scratch the surface in telling about them. The patrols recounted in the preceding pages give the firsthand stories of what our submariners endured and accomplished in the earlier months of the war. Those were the months when the going was toughest and the fate of our nation hung in the balance. Those were the months when our well- prepared and daring undersea fleet—our major hope and far-flung line of defense—stood off the Japanese and gave our Navy an opportunity to build and restore its power on the surface and in the air. It is a tribute to the skill of our men in the submarines that, during the first fourteen months of the war, the enemy was able to sink only three of our ships. Aside from the fact that more submarines were in action, the increasing losses of our Submarine Service were, ironically, to some extent due to its effectiveness.

As the Japanese shipping was whittled down, it became necessary for our submarines to venture farther into heavily guarded areas, to take more daring chances, in order to find targets for their torpedoes, with a consequent increase in losses by enemy action.

In the closing days of the war, when our mighty battle fleets moved in close to the shores of the Japanese homeland and hurled tons of shells in direct bombardment of enemy defenses, the American public was amazed that they had been able to penetrate the heavy belt of mines with which the Japanese were known to have lined their coasts.

The answer was—our submarines! Sixteen of our submarines, with secret equipment, made twenty-five passages through the thousands of mines. They cleared the way for our heavy surface warships to approach the enemy coast. And in making these passages not one of our minesweeping submarines was lost, although one of them was caught inside the minefields and sunk by a destroyer's depth charge.

This mass operation by submarines was the natural outcome of the undersea tactics developed by the Navy as soon as sufficient submarines had been built. Because their numbers were so few at the start, in almost all instances our submarines played a lone hand on their patrols. Later, however, we took a leaf from the book of the Germans, who had brought so-called "wolf-pack" submarine operation to a high point of effectiveness. In the words of Admiral Lockwood, "we went the Germans one better" with our wolf packs. Squadrons of our submarines blanketed large areas of the Pacific and adjoining waters. It was a lucky enemy ship, indeed, that was able to get through. And instead of having to fend off attacks by lone submarines, often unhappy Japanese vessels found themselves beset from many directions at once by our hard-hitting submarines.

The rescue of some of the officers and men of the submarine U.S.S. *Sculpin* from Japanese prison camps brought to light an instance of individual heroism and devotion to duty that was not surpassed in the war. It typifies the spirit of the whole Submarine Service. Lieutenant George E. Brown told the story of "the man who knew too much."

The *Sculpin* was the flagship of Captain John Cromwell, USN, 43-year-old submarine division commander, on November 18, 1943. (The operation of a flagship is the responsibility of the ship's regular officers; the flag officer aboard is more or less of a "guest" in respect to that.) The American submarine had been trailing an enemy convoy when, just as she maneuvered into position to launch her torpedoes, she was sighted.

"We went down," Lieutenant Brown said, "and waited an hour. Then we surfaced right in front of a Jap destroyer that had been left there as a 'sleeper.' Twice depth-charge attacks damaged us. Two more strings of depth bombs cracked the torpedo tubes and jammed most of the outboard vents and sea valves.

"We were through then, but our captain decided to surface and fight it out. After about twenty salvos had been exchanged, the Japs put two shells through the conning tower, killing all senior officers. "Their deaths left me in charge," Lieutenant Brown said. "I told Captain Cromwell I was going to scuttle. He said: 'Go ahead, but I can't come with you because I know too much and don't want to get into Jap hands'."

The submarine was scuttled. The survivors among her crew and officers took to the water—all except Captain Cromwell. Fearing that torture might wring from him information that would aid the enemy, he went down with the *Sculpin*.

The future of the submarine as an instrument of war is, of course, purely a matter of speculation. Technical and scientific advances are taking place with such startling speed that any prediction is at best little more than a guess. Nevertheless, there are indications that in the atomic age the importance of undersea ships will be vastly increased. Certainly our Submarine Command thinks so. There are indications, too, that the Navy as a whole is laying its future plans with that idea in mind. And the atomic scientists themselves would appear to support the Navy view.

Dr. Alvin M. Weinberg, chief of the theoretical physics section of Clinton Laboratories in the Oak Ridge, Tennessee, atomic bomb plant, visions submarines powered by atomic fuel traveling a thousand feet underwater as fast as our surface ships travel today.

Speaking of the atomic fire at the Hanford, Washington, atom bomb plant, which burns without oxygen, Dr. Weinberg said, "Here is an ideal fuel for use in a submarine; with it a ship can travel as fast underwater as on the surface." He pointed out that one pound of fissionable material (the source of atomic power) releases as much energy as a million pounds of ordinary fuel.

"Should an atomic war break out," said Dr. Weinberg, "the safest place on this tortured planet will be deep below the surface of the ocean."

THE END

American Propaganda poster lampooning 'the Big 3' – Hitler, Mussolini, and Hirohito. Image: U.S. National Archives and Records Administration

Made in United States
Orlando, FL
18 January 2022

13662789R00096